WINTER CREEK

THE *CREDO* SERIES

A *credo* is a statement of belief, an assertion of deep conviction. The *Credo* series offers contemporary American writers whose work emphasizes the natural world and the human community the opportunity to discuss their essential goals, concerns, and practices. Each volume presents an individual writer's *credo,* his or her investigation of what it means to write about human experience and society in the context of the more-than-human world, as well as a biographical profile and complete bibliography of the author's published work. The *Credo* series offers some of our best writers an opportunity to speak to the fluid and subtle issues of rapidly changing technology, social structure, and environmental conditions.

WINTER CREEK

ONE WRITER'S NATURAL HISTORY

JOHN DANIEL

Scott Slovic, *Credo* Series Editor

Credo

MILKWEED EDITIONS

Published 2002 by Milkweed Editions
Printed in Canada
Cover image © 2000 Derke/O'Hara/Stone
Cover design by Dale Cooney
The text of this book is set in Stone Serif.
02 03 04 05 06   5 4 3 2 1
First Edition

Milkweed Editions, a nonprofit publisher, gratefully acknowledges support from our World As Home funder, Reader's Legacy underwriter Elly Sturgis. Other support has been provided by the Bush Foundation; General Mills Foundation; Marshall Field's Project Imagine with support from the Target Foundation and Target Stores; McKnight Foundation; Minnesota State Arts Board through an appropriation by the Minnesota State Legislature and a grant from the National Endowment for the Arts, and a grant from Wells Fargo Foundation Minnesota; St. Paul Companies, Inc.; and generous individuals.

Library of Congress Cataloging-in-Publication Data

Daniel, John, 1948–
    Winter creek : one writer's natural history / John Daniel. — 1st ed.
        p.   cm. — (Credo)
    Includes bibliographical references.
    ISBN 1-57131-266-8 (pbk. : alk. paper)
    1. Daniel, John, 1948– 2. Poets, American—20th century—
Biography.   3. Naturalists—United States—Biography.   4. Northwest,
Pacific—Biography.   I. Title.   II. Credo series (Minneapolis, Minn.)
    PS3554.A5534 Z463 2002
    811'.54—dc21
                                                                2002002014

This book is printed on acid-free, recycled paper.

For Wendell Berry

WINTER CREEK

Winter Creek

Winter Creek

ONE WRITER'S NATURAL HISTORY

by John Daniel

Wakening

As a boy growing up in what were then the semirural outskirts of Washington, D.C., I was drawn to the natural world, but not to any extraordinary degree. I often poked around the nameless little creek that ran in a vale between two sections of our suburb, catching frogs and water striders, trying to net minnows in my white t-shirt, turning over stones to look for crayfish. Now and then, by myself or with a friend or two, I ventured down to the towpath of the Chesapeake and Ohio Canal, long abandoned by commerce, and beyond the canal to the muddy sloughs and side channels of the Potomac River. We went to fish, usually, but sometimes we simply explored, wandering the sycamore forests as if we were the first white people ever to walk there. The river was hard on that fantasy. Cans and bottles were everywhere, along with hunks of sodden packaging, the odd shoe or rag of clothing, even bedsprings and other rusted works of metal embedded in the Potomac's mud.

Our pioneering expeditions usually devolved into junk hunts.

The river ran brown and sometimes stunk. Gobs of matter drifted by that looked like shit and no doubt were. The word "polluted" entered my vocabulary early in grade school, always in reference to the Potomac. I don't recall ever being told or thinking about why or how the pollution occurred. The river was simply "polluted," as if that quality were part of its nature. I knew little of where the Potomac came from or what life lived in it, apart from the catfish and smallmouth bass I fished for. My friends and I knew the river's legendry better than we knew the river. It was said, for instance, that young George Washington had thrown a silver dollar clear across the Potomac. We derided that story. The river was far too wide, and even if George had had the arm to do it, why would he have thrown away a dollar? Nobody could have been that stupid, even two hundred years ago.

My pursuits were mainly the ordinary pursuits of suburban boys in the 1950s and early 60s—food, baseball, bicycles (with playing cards clothespinned to flap loudly against the spokes), and TV. My friends and I spent our ample leisure time in and around one another's homes, trading baseball cards, playing games, fooling around. We were forever forming clubs and cliques, little factions that squabbled among themselves for a day or two, then reunited and redivided into a new balance of power. We played war a lot. Wearing real helmet liners from army surplus stores, we stalked and ambushed one another, blasting away with fake rifles and the shrillest sound effects our windpipes could supply. Then we argued about who was dead and who wasn't.

On weekends, or any day during summer, it was my habit to pedal my red J. C. Higgins bicycle to Dickerson's Store to buy a few packs of baseball cards. On my way home I stopped at a certain grassy slope along the trolley tracks that led into Washington, and there I lay in the sun and opened my cards. I loved the crisp bright smell they gave off, a blend of ink and bubblegum. The information on the backs of the cards was my favorite reading. When I had them inventoried and had admired the admirable players and noted the others, I put the cards aside, took from my pocket a pencil and a folded piece of paper, and wrote a poem. I'd write a line, erase to make a change if I needed to, write another line. A poem might take me ten minutes or half an hour. One, I remember, was about watching a parade. Another was about my birthday. The poems delighted my aunts, and perhaps my parents too, though I don't remember that.

I can't recall how I first came to write poems, or when. It was just something I did. Lounging on the hillside, I liked the way the yellow pencil felt against the paper. When stuck for a word or phrase I sometimes chewed the pencil, as if to bite from it the missing language. I liked the white, blue-lined notebook paper bright with sun, the daydreamy haze I moved into and out of. I liked making rhymes. I think I knew, despite my aunts' effusions, that my poems were nothing special, but writing them gave me a mild satisfaction. Creative writing is thought of as self-expression, and it is, but its essence is the making of language into something whole, the way a sculptor makes a wholeness of clay or bronze. A poet, even a ten-year-old writing formulaic verses about a parade, is a maker more than anything else. I liked riding home with a new poem in the right front pocket of my pants.

I wasn't yet a poet, of course. I found subjects to write about, but my subject had not yet found me. I never wrote of one particular oddness in my young life, an oddness that I now understand as the first calling of my subject. I thought of it as too silly-seeming to share with friends or family, and too hard to tell about in any case. Some mornings I would wake earlier than usual to the light of dawn in my window and birdsong sounding from the yard. I would wonder how long the first bird had been singing before I'd awakened, and with that question came a hunger for I didn't know what. In my mind I ran down the list of my favorite foods—Raisin Bran, my father's raised buckwheat pancakes with smoked sausage, rare sirloin steak from the barbecue, my mother's strawberry shortcake—but none of them matched my hunger, and neither did any of the activities—fishing or playing baseball or going to double-feature movies—that usually gave me pleasure. As I worked through the inventory of possibilities, I always came to the conclusion—which I recognized as somehow important, as maybe defining me in a distinct way—that what I hungered for was something I had not yet tasted, something hinted in the songs of birds but not the songs themselves, something hidden outside in the cool morning if it existed in the world at all, something unheard, unseen, that could be mine if only I could name it.

I often preferred reading a book to playing with friends. Sometimes I even faked reading in order to remain alone.

Once I got rid of Bobby Bradley, my best friend, by feigning an avid interest in Macaulay's *History of England*. The text was not compelling, but the physical book was. I admired the rough edges of the pages, the hard gray covers embossed with opulent lettering, the musty fresh smell that filled my nose when I buried it in the open spine. Books were all around our house, all kinds of books, from nice sets of Shakespeare and Francis Parkman to cheap paperback novels with lurid (for the 1950s) covers. It was commonplace to see my parents reading, my father in his maple rocking chair, my mother in the morris chair or on the sofa. I grew up understanding that books were substantial things and that reading them was something valid and valuable.

Sometimes, usually after a few drinks, my father would read out loud in his deep voice from Shakespeare or the Bible. (He called himself an agnostic, but he had once been a seminarian and he loved the language of the King James.) My father was something of an orator by trade, a career industrial union organizer whose most powerful tool was his voice. Once, when I was very young, he took me along on a trip and I heard him speak. I saw how the workers listened to him. His voice and gesturing hands seemed to have them under a spell, and afterward some of them crowded up to shake his hand. I don't remember specifically, but I must have desired to be like him, to have his power for my own. How could I not have? And I must have wished for his way of telling stories, too. I often watched and listened as he told of picket line scuffles and other anecdotes his friends might have heard before, but they responded as if hearing them for the first time, because the telling was so vivid and the teller so alive and delighted with his tale.

Interspersed with classical music and jazz, songs of the labor movement frequently were playing on our hi-fi, songs such as "Joe Hill," "Union Maid," "Which Side Are You On?," "Solidarity Forever." Those were the hymns of our unreligious household, songs of truth outlasting death, of knowing what you believe and having the courage to stand for it, of drawing strength from others and fortifying them with your own. My father also liked to play recordings of newscasts of historic events, some narrated by Edward R. Murrow in his tightly controlled baritone. As I grew up the living room sounded with the voices of Churchill and FDR, of Calvin Coolidge averring that the business of America was business, of an anguished radio reporter describing the Hindenburg airship collapsing in flames. And poetry. My father was as fond of Dylan Thomas as he was of Beethoven, and I can still hear those bold Welsh enunciations ringing at volume through the rooms of the house—*Now as I was young and easy under the apple boughs*—to the metronomic accompaniment of a loud scratch on the record.

My mother's taste ran more to e. e. cummings and the avant-garde. She would borrow recordings from the library and play them when my father wasn't around. I remember cummings's high-pitched voice, the way he virtually sang his lines: *i thank You God for most this amaaaazing day.* My parents argued once about a poem by Ralph Hodgson, "Time, You Old Gypsy Man." My father thought it was profound; my mother thought it was corny. I knew they were capable of arguing about anything, but this was the first time I'd heard them argue about literature. I had assumed that all grownups felt the same about stuff in books, that it was all considered good by everyone.

My parents' arguments weren't often so civil and weren't usually about poetry. They were loud, inflamed, and frequent. I hated them, and hated my parents for having them, but I learned from those arguments too. At school it was common for any of us to reply to a taunt with *Sticks and stones can break my bones, but names can never hurt me.* I said it myself at times, but I knew it wasn't true. I knew, listening in my bed, or at the shut bedroom door if the argument seemed especially volatile, that words intended to hurt could hurt, did hurt, and set the hurt loose throughout the house. It may be wishful thinking, but it's possible that understanding that power of language may have heightened my interest in its other, more beneficial, powers.

Ours was a home in which language lived, and I believe I carry all that language with me, mingled with the rest of my experience like compost in a bottomless bin. All of us carry a rich lode of it. I would be thirty before I considered myself a writer, but all the while leading up to that age the compost was working, forming horizons of soil beneath the light of consciousness, stirring with unknown life. Writers till that soil, and though they might recognize very little of what they have read and what they have heard in the growings they coax into being, it's all there, every phrase and syllable, every accent and inflection. They can say very little in honesty about where this or that work came from. Everything they raise is nourished by the whole soil.

On the coast of Maine, where our family usually stayed at my grandfather's summer home a few weeks every year, my brother and I fished with handlines from a small floating wharf at the end of a pier. We baited our hooks with clams we'd dug at low tide from the rocky, seaweedy beach below the house. The clams were unsafe for eating, contaminated by raw sewage piped directly into Frenchman's Bay from the waterfront homes, including my grandfather's. (I don't recall hearing the term "polluted" in reference to the clams—probably, I see now, because in this case the taint came from us.) For pollock, shiny silvery fish up to a foot or so long, we used most of a clam for bait and lowered our weighted lines fifteen or twenty feet. We had to be alert, standing or kneeling at the edge of the wharf with the line in an outstretched hand, ready to jerk upward the instant a sharp tug shot up the line. If pollock were around, they'd hit. We caught them in flurries, excitedly raising them hand over hand, dehooking them into a bucket of seawater and rebaiting our lines with trembling fingers, eager for the next hard bite.

For flounder, the better fish for eating, we worked differently. We used a smaller hook, better suited to the flounder's narrow, delicate mouth, baited it with a tender clam stomach, and lowered it—carefully, so as not to lose the bait—to the bottom of the bay. Pulling up just a few inches to tauten the line, we waited. This was a more meditative fishing, more an exercise of faith. My brother was better at it. As I crouched with line in hand

I struggled against distraction by trying to visualize a flounder approaching the bait, his flat form wriggling along the bottom, brown above, pale below. They're like us, I remember thinking. They live on land, their land's just underwater.

But I knew very well that the flounder was not like us, that the flounder was strangeness itself. I knew from my mother that the baby flounder began as a normal upright fish, but that one eye migrated from one side of its head to the other, and then the side with the eyes became the upper side when the flounder flopped over and became, for the rest of its life, a flatfish. That was the oddest fact of natural history I knew as a kid, and it's the oddest I know today.

I think it was that strangeness, more than the prospect of a tasty dinner, that kept me kneeling on the wharf those days when I had the patience, waiting for the slight, tentative, singular tug of the flounder's mouth at the bottom of the bay. (The mouth was twisted, as if it had tried to convert from upright to flat but had got caught between.) For some reason, fishing for flounder mattered a lot. It felt close to prayer at times, closer than anything I knew. I poured my concentration down the braided line, hoping for a sign from that other world, to be recognized by the mystery I couldn't see—and, if I was alert and quick enough, to feel its vibrant, darting life, to draw it to the surface with my own hands. That was always the best, raising the unseen strangeness, its charge traveling up my arms and all through me, before it flopped on the painted wharf and splashed for a while in the bucket.

In Louisiana once, on a family vacation, I went bass

fishing early one morning with a friend of my father's. He guided the boat through the quiet, black-water bayous, telling me where to cast my plastic worm—there, by those lily pads, now by that big-kneed cypress. I was hitting the spots pretty well but getting no strikes.

"I don't know why you're not catchin' a fish," my father's friend said after a while. He looked thoughtful. "Maybe you're not holdin' your mouth right."

I couldn't get it out of my mind the rest of the morning. I cast my worm with a normal smile, a one-sided smile, lips open, lips closed, tongue between teeth, teeth on lower lip, then forgot about my mouth, then remembered and tried all the positions again and thought up some more.

Late in the morning I was startled by a strike as I reeled in my worm, and eventually I hoisted a nice largemouth into the boat. "Yeah!" I yelled. Getting the hook out of the fish's mouth, I tried to remember. I must have looked troubled, because as we cruised in for the day, the wind washing over us, my father's friend called from the stern, "I can tell you. I was watchin'."

"How was I holding it?"

"You were holdin' it just right," he said.

At home I fished and dreamed about fishing. I studied issues of *Sports Afield* and *Outdoor Life,* fantasizing about muskellunge in northern lakes, steelhead and salmon in western rivers I had never seen. I saved money to buy lures, a tackle box, a new spinning reel. I sent away for materials and constructed my own rod, mounting the line guides on the fiberglass blank with precise tight wraps of brightly colored thread followed by several coats of lacquer. I spent hours in the backyard casting a small lead sinker into a bushel basket from farther and farther away.

I never caught much in the Potomac. Rivers are hard to know how to fish, especially big rivers, and I had no guide or boat. Then in 1960 my parents bought a weekend place, an old cabin on the Blue Ridge of northern Virginia, and I found my home waters. Several nearby farm ponds were stocked with bluegills and largemouth bass. I fished early in the morning, late in the evening, sometimes in the middle of the day. Bluegills were easy, like the pollock in Maine. Worms, grasshoppers, artificial flies, little spinners, even purple pokeweed berries worked for bluegills. I scorned their feeble intelligence and aimed my ambition at the bass. Worms and other bait didn't do the trick because a bluegill would always get to it first. I tried big spinners, and then surface plugs, lures designed to mimic crippled frogs or other bass prey. I cast my first plug early one morning as mist was rising from the water, and just as the plug hit the surface the pond erupted beneath it in an angry swirl, bouncing the plug into the air. I reeled in, my knees shaky.

"Come on," I said. "Come on, please."

I cast and cast through the morning, holding my mouth every way I could imagine. By noon, hungry and sleepy in the hot sun, I was letting the plug drift on the pond for long intervals as my mind did the same. The plug was no more than ten feet from shore when it was swallowed in a huge splash and my rod bent double. I felt the power, two or three lunging surges, before the monofilament line snapped. I trudged back to our cabin, miserable at losing the fish and leaving him with a two-inch hunk of plastic and metal in his mouth.

A couple of years later I told a farmhand the story, and he nodded. "I seen that daddy," he told me. "Got a big ol' bug in his jaw. He's a good one."

I never did catch that fish, but I did catch others. I had the most luck with a yellow diving plug called a Heddon Sonic. I experimented with various retrieves and one day found the right one. I cast, let the plug sink to the bottom, then drew it toward me with hard sideward sweeps of the rod, pausing a couple of seconds between sweeps. In the middle of one sweep my rod stopped dead. I thought I had snagged bottom, but then bottom moved, dragging line from my reel, and in a few minutes I was lifting a three-pound bass in my left hand, his raspy teeth drawing blood from my fingers. I caught two more the same way and hiked home lugging ten pounds of bass on my stringer. It was the happiest day of my life.

I fished in those years with a concentration I gave nothing else. I cast and cast in a trance of hopeful expectancy, which in time, with no action, became supplication and eventually a whiny petulance, but which always renewed itself with each fresh start on a new day. Years later, when I began to write poems, the emotional rhythm would feel familiar—the casting forth, trying to imagine what I couldn't yet see, the sense that it was there, waiting, if only I could find it. Alertness, distraction, alertness again. The sense that somehow, though I couldn't say why, it mattered very much. The dull frustration of hours and days when nothing was hitting. The almost frightened enthusiasm when I felt a nibble, and the surprise, each time, when the nibble became something sustained, a bright resistance showing itself in glints, a flashing protean form that I worked nearer and nearer and finally drew from the depths if I was patient and lucky.

Our cabin sat in a hollow along the eastern base of the Blue Ridge, on land that had been farmed at one time and now was going back to hardwood forest. Ghosts of old roads lined the woods, forming trails through the tangled ground cover of honeysuckle and other vines, shrubs, and briars. At first I hiked within a mile or two of the cabin, usually with my mother. It was she who had fallen in love with the place and arranged to buy it. She lit up when we left town for the cabin. She wasn't especially knowledgeable of nature—I don't remember her teaching me to identify plants and animals—but she had an affinity for it. She responded with interest and a spirit of bright sympathy for the creatures and sounds and stillnesses of the woods. Surely we all have that potential—we are of the nature we are born to, wild as any woodpecker—but it can stifle, lie dormant. I was lucky to have a place and a parent to stir it in me.

We often walked down a grassy lane and up across a slope through trees and undergrowth to the grave of Tolamiah Rodes, the man who built the original structure of our cabin in the 1830s. The grave was marked by an almost indecipherable headstone tilted loosely among rocks. I wanted to know all about Tolamiah Rodes, what he had done, what his life had been like. I wanted to know about the few ruins that spotted the woods, tumbledown stone foundations with weathered scraps of carpentry still standing. We learned only a little from a local farmer. It was said that Tolamiah's young wife had been taken by a mountain lion, after which Tolamiah kept to himself. One building had been his tannery. Its stone-lined cellar, cut into the hillside, was so dank and dark I wouldn't go in.

When I walked alone I tramped the old roads, scanning for further signs of human habitation. I stopped at likely places to poke the ground with my stick. I found little—a broken jar, a square nail—but I hiked and rummaged with a recurrent hope that some momentous discovery awaited me. A cache of gold coins, maybe. A cannon from the Civil War. A human skeleton in a cave propped next to a note scratched into stone. Except for the infrequent box turtle or blacksnake, the occasional climbable tree or swingable vine, the woods as woods didn't hold my interest long. Trees were only trees, rocks were rocks.

Even as I pursued my fantasies, though, the nature of the place was working on me. One day my mother took me to a spot she had found not far from the cabin, a small jumble of slabby stones encrusted with dry moss.

"Sit there," she said.

I sat and looked at her. "What for?"

"Listen," she said, raising a finger to her lips.

I heard nothing, then something. A lulling whisper, changeful, like far-off wind. I looked around at the forest, still and silent in the afternoon heat. My mother smiled. I closed my eyes and lowered my head, concentrating. Then I leaned over and put my ear to the rocks.

"It's a river!" I yelled. "Where's it from?"

"Nowhere I know, child," said my mother. "It must come down the mountain. It feeds our spring, I suppose."

It stunned me to think of a stream flowing underground, giving no sign of itself above. In the months that followed I often stopped at the patch of stones to listen. Once I curled down among the stones, making myself comfortable as only a kid can do, and listened a long time to the secret waters moving down the mountainside, murmuring in darkness in a voice that seemed always on the verge of speech. When I woke I felt myself returning from far away.

As I got older I explored up the Blue Ridge, up the dirt lane that led to a few houses above ours and then up a short connecting path to the Appalachian Trail, which follows the crest of the ridge. It stirred me to stand on a pathway that could take me north to Maine or south to Georgia, to imagine walking to those far places. I hiked short distances along the trail, catching glimpses through pines and hardwoods of the territory to the west, the Shenandoah Valley and the Allegheny Mountains.

One morning, when I was fourteen, I set out to explore farther north on the Appalachian Trail than I had before, and I took a more ambitious route to the ridge top. Instead of following the dirt lane and the connecting trail, I hiked overland, directly up the slope from the cabin. I knew I could make it to the top, and I knew that once there I couldn't miss the trail. I told my mother where I was going but not how.

It was a hot morning. The climb was brushy and brambly, and I soon felt sorry for myself. And scared, because I didn't know where I was and nobody else did either. But eventually the pitch of the mountainside eased, and the thickets I'd been fighting gave way to a field of small gray boulders. I stopped for a drink of water, then shouldered my knapsack and hopped ahead from one boulder to another, making good time and regaining my spirit. In the middle of the boulder field, I heard a quick buzz beneath me. I jumped to the next boulder and another buzz came, then another. I froze. I saw no movement, nothing but boulders in sunlight, and the whole bright strew of them seemed to be buzzing around me.

I had seen one rattlesnake in my life, thick as my arm and nearly as long as I was tall, sliding through high grass near the cabin. From TV or *National Geographic* I had an image of jaws gaping unnaturally wide, a flickering black tongue, long fangs curved inward. I tried to quiet my shaking knees, to stand as still and light and thin as I could. It alarms me now how guilty I felt that nobody knew where I was, as if the whole thing were my own fault, a punishment for doing wrong. I didn't know if I believed in God, but I was scared enough to want to. I vowed I'd be good. I'd never leave the trail again. I shifted my feet and instantly heard a buzz. I thought I saw motion between two boulders.

I remember feeling emptied of everything but my fear, my breathing. The stones were radiant with clarity. I saw every irregularity and scruff of moss, every edge and smoothness, every sparkle that made each stone just so. I wasn't looking for this, but I saw it. And I saw the hollows and canyons of shadow between the stones, the perfect black depths they rested in. Nothing moved. I felt strangely separate from myself, calm and afraid at the same time. A squirrel rustled in a tree over on the shore of safety.

I looked for a path of boulders a step or short jump

apart, not up or down but across the slope. Stones that stood higher than others but flat enough for my boots to grip. Stones that looked like they wouldn't wobble. I tested each one, pushed against it with my vision. I traded one for another, traded back, and all the while I was aware of the blue sky and felt it around me. A breeze came up, cold through my damp t-shirt. I bent from my waist, slowly, and tightened first my left boot laces, then my right. Very deliberately, I made myself smile and hold the smile. And I jumped.

My legs took over and the plan was gone. I bounded wildly, too fast to think, and if I touched off any buzzes they were drowned in the roaring of my fear. Once I slipped and my left foot plunged into shadow. I vaulted up, crying out, and danced from stone to stone with a nimbleness that someone, me but not me, was enjoying. I didn't stop when I reached the trees but ran across the limb-littered forest floor to a place where I could see bare ground. There I yanked up my pant leg to see what had hurt me. My shin was red and bleeding. I'd barked it when I slipped, but I thought I saw twin fang marks too, the leg beginning to swell. I launched myself up the mountain in a new panic. If I could make it to the Appalachian Trail, someone might find me. *Just let me make it,* I pleaded.

I made it, and I was no longer running and stumbling when I did. Fatigue had quickly exhausted my panic, and the news from my leg, though painful, was a kind of hurt I knew. I felt sheepish about the ruckus I'd put myself through, grateful that only snakes and trees had witnessed it. I decided I wouldn't tell my mother. I would say only that I had slipped and scraped my leg.

I hiked north, as I had originally intended, and eventually came to an open height, a stone outcrop where thick hardwoods gave way to sparse pines. I drank from my canteen, ate my sandwiches, and looked westward at a landscape I had never seen before in unobstructed wholeness. The brown Shenandoah looped evenly through patched forest and farmland, and beyond the river the Allegheny Mountains ranged away into a hazy distance, ridge after folded blue ridge.

I sat, my arms around my knees, watching with a wild exultation. The wind sang in the pines and sang in me. I took out paper and pencil after a while and started a poem, the first I had written about a landscape and the first about something I was directly observing. Everything I saw, everything I heard and smelled, had the perfect clarity of the boulders when I'd stood and studied them. Everything seemed both strange and familiar.

I wrote a sentence and stared at it on the page: *The world is a dream, and the dream is true.* The slow Shenandoah, the blue Alleghenies, the wind with its pine scent and tune of yearning, the bright crag where I sat, the sunny boulders where I'd stood, the rattlesnakes unseen in their dark chambers, the land lying west where I knew I would live someday—all of it was true, and the strangest thing was that *I* was true, that somehow I was there, apart from it and a part of it at the same time.

Eventually, when the sun was starting to drift low, I got up and headed home. I took the easy way, down the connecting path to the dirt lane, but I knew I would break my vow never to leave the trail again. I'd made the vow only because I was scared. I wasn't bound to it.

I was bound only to the truth of what I had seen and the pain of my scraped leg. They were the same somehow. I carried them like a secret I had found, a secret that was mine to keep.

There's a short poem by Walt Whitman, "Beginning My Studies," that I first came upon in my midthirties. I read it with a shock of affinity:

> Beginning my studies the first step pleas'd me
> so much,
> The mere fact consciousness, these forms, the
> power of motion,
> The least insect or animal, the senses, eyesight,
> love,
> The first step I say awed me and pleas'd me so
> much,
> I have hardly gone and hardly wish'd to go any
> farther,
> But stop and loiter all the time to sing it in ec-
> static songs.

I instantly recognized myself as one who has hardly gone and hardly wishes to go farther than the fact of consciousness. From that day when I looked west from the Blue Ridge into the strange and familiar dream of the world and felt its truth, I've been possessed by a twofold riddle. The world did not have to be, yet here it is. And nothing in the world had to be aware of the world or of itself, yet here we are.

To wonder at that double miracle, to praise it, to sing it in songs, has not been the only motive of my work in writing but has been the deepest and most persistent. I'm still the kid who hollered, "It's a river!

Where's it from?" I understand now—and knew even then, I suppose—that neither I nor anyone else can know where the river of being comes from or why it flows or where, if anywhere, it may be going. It is enough, it is plenty, to be alive in its flowing, to glimpse some of its beauties and terrors, to find forms of language for some of what I glimpse. I believe, with Thoreau, that Nature is the greater and more perfect art, the art of God. My human art is one small way of answering, in gratitude, the incalculable gift of being.

WEST

I saw the West for the first time in 1953, when my father's work in the labor movement took us to Denver for a year. I was five. The only landscape I really got to know was our ample side yard on South Fillmore Street, where two big cottonwoods stood. I remember their gray ridgy bark and my confusion about their name—if cotton was pants and shirts, what did it have to do with trees? My sharpest memory from Denver is of the first great natural act to visit my life, a summer hailstorm. My brother, Jim, had a football helmet, and wearing that we took turns ducking out into the pelting stones, which were about the size of grapes and made a clattering racket on the helmet that drove us delirious with pleasure. We whooped and danced, the ice stones stinging our arms and shoulders, and afterward, in warm sunshine, I hauled pail after pail of the bright nuggets and heaped them high, a treasure of melting wealth.

In 1954 my father was promoted to a Washington, D.C., assignment, and we left Colorado. Before driving east we toured around the mountain West—Rocky Mountain National Park, the Tetons, Yellowstone, the Bighorns, the Black Hills. I've got scores of black-and-white snapshots of my brother and me at those places and many others, usually standing next to a sign marking a historical site or sitting at the base of a monument. My father appreciated natural beauty and always gardened and fed the songbirds wherever we lived, but he valued the landscape highest as the stage and scenery for human dramas. He had a passion for history. He loved the mountain men, the saga of the westward expansion, the histories of the Indian wars. He told us stories of the places we saw. My first appreciation of the open land, as settings hallowed by battles, by footsteps, by human triumph and tragedy, came from him.

I felt the land directly, too. At Little Bighorn I was awed by the afternoon heat, which was dry, gusty, and immense, a heat that towered and swelled, that ranged as wide as the expansive sky. I was giddy with sun and distance. On the highway later, we saw tumbleweeds on the move. I insisted we stop so that I could pick one out to take east with us. My parents humored me, found a place for it in the trunk. I kept it in my room in our new house in Maryland, and when Christmas came I decorated my prize weed with tinsel and paper figures and had my own Christmas tree. Maybe I knew even then that I belonged in the West.

I certainly knew it nine years later, on another cross-country drive. On that trip I saw the Grand Canyon and the Sierra Nevada for the first time, but the sight that most captivated me was nothing of nature. In San Francisco the towers and graceful cabled curves of the Golden Gate Bridge, brilliant red-orange against the deep blue sky, struck my vision like a bolt of happiness. As we left the city, driving east past Oakland and Berkeley, I kept looking back at the bridge in the distance behind. Doris Day was singing "Que Sera, Sera" on the car radio. *"Whatever will be, will be. . . ."* This is where I'll be, I said to myself.

On that second journey through the West I began to realize how little of the land we were seeing as we followed our track of pavement, stopping at viewpoints and historic sites, holing up in motels at night. I watched the passing edges of forest and big windy spaces and yearned to stop, to enter, to know their secrets. I had been reading, on my father's recommendation, Bernard DeVoto's great trilogy on the westward expansion—*The Course of Empire, Across the Wide Missouri,* and *The Year of Decision: 1846.* My imagination was charged. With the miles rolling by I fantasized myself as a mountain man, as Lewis or Clark, or as just me but changed— waving good-bye to my family, running from the car and highway up a grassy embankment and disappearing into the mountains. Sometimes I ran with Karen Jaeger, the girl I sat next to in ninth-grade Latin. Sometimes I ran alone.

The only wilderness I knew in my grade school years was Alaska. I had shipped up the Inside Passage to Juneau, worked my way to Skagway, strained and sweated over Chilkoot Pass with a hundred-pound pack on my back, looked out for myself in the saloons of Whitehorse, and trekked the Yukon interior in search of adventure and the rich paystreaks. I had learned to judge the degree of cold by the crackle of my spit in the air, to treat my dogs as though my life depended on them (because it did), and never to build a fire beneath snowy boughs. Jack London taught me those things, and he wakened something else in me. Before I ever hiked or camped or climbed in wild country, I had been stirred by its elemental immensity. I had been touched by the beauty of needle-tree forests I had never seen, bright rivers flowing among nameless peaks, the howls of wolves, the shimmering fire of the night sky. Someone gave me a science book for young readers about the interactions of plants and animals, a 1950s ecology primer that no doubt was ahead of its time. I put it aside in boredom, but *The Call of the Wild, White Fang,* and *Smoke Bellew* I consumed with passion, and it was the Alaskan landscape, along with the dogs, that excited me.

In high school a teacher lent me a thin paperback of Robinson Jeffers's poems, *The Beginning and the End,* and later his *Selected Poems.* I had read little poetry and had long since stopped writing it, but Jeffers was compelling. He came from the page unbeautified, direct, but oracular, as if he *knew.* He made his storm-pummeled landscape vivid (even the names seemed wildly beautiful—Point Lobos, Sur Rivers, Santa Cruz), but it was his perspective that got me. He evoked a violently grand cosmos that had formed through unthinkable reaches of time and somehow engendered earth and sea and the clarity of a hawk's vision. He made human history and human achievement—what I'd been studying in school for twelve years—seem small and inconsequential, doomed in any case by our self-involved pettiness and warfare. I wasn't sure he was right, but doom in one form or another is irresistibly attractive to an adolescent. It thrilled me that Jeffers said he'd sooner kill a man than a hawk. I didn't believe him, but he sounded like no one else in my reading.

So I guess I'd been primed to love the western wilds well before I drove my mother's Jeep to Portland, Oregon, in 1966 to begin studies at Reed College. I'd never been to Oregon, which at the time I must have pronounced "ARE-uh-GAHN," and for two years I saw little of its landscape, let alone its wilds. Being a student can be bad for your health if you take it too seriously.

It keeps you indoors too much and your mind too busy with abstractions. The purpose of an education should be to discover what your life most needs for its nourishment, but all too easily you can wind up eating the menu and never quite getting to the meal. The time I didn't spend in class I spent reading, reading, and writing papers. The time I didn't spend reading and writing I spent smoking dope, talking with friends, listening to rock at high volume, and brooding about the glacial progress of my sexual life. At Reed the only outdoor place I regularly visited was the little wooded stream course Reedies call the Canyon. We hid our stashes of drugs there. The great Northwest, for all I glimpsed of it, was mist and rain, green fields and fronts of forest passing in the frame of a wet car window.

But there were moments. At some point in the fall of my freshman year, a shot of lightning exploded the top of one of the tallest trees on campus, a solitary Douglas fir, and turned it into a flaming torch. I wasn't lucky enough to see the strike, but I did come along in time to watch yellow flames blazing in the top of a tall dark tree. "This," I said to myself, "is a cool place." My enthusiasm waxed further a year later when a ripping windstorm blew in off the Pacific. On campus with friends, I watched trees snapping and tumbling on the other side of the river in southwest Portland, taking down power lines and popping a transformer now and then with a hail of sparks. Unthreatened ourselves, we whooped and cheered the wind on. Robinson Jeffers, somewhere beyond the material world, was having a very good day.

And then once, hitchhiking back to Portland from

San Francisco, my friend Danny and I were stranded half the night on Interstate 5 in northern California. It was clear and brutally cold, the freeway almost deserted. The granite cliffs of Castle Crags stood west of us, flooded with moon, and above us to the north loomed the snowy ghost of Mount Shasta. We hunched and jogged and stamped our feet, and somehow our misery made moon and crags and mountain more intensely beautiful. There was glory and solemnity everywhere. We shivered there for hours before an 18-wheeler's brake lights popped on and we heard the happy decelerating tune of its jake brake. We shouted and ran stiffly after it, our interstate angel of mercy.

More than thirty years after the fact, I scarcely recollect what Danny and I had been doing in San Francisco. Those memories have blurred, blended with others. But the long vigil on an empty freeway—moon and crags, Shasta's luminous specter, the colossal, humbling cold—I recall in singular clarity. That night, for the first time, I was in the presence of the western land. I felt a joy, not secondhand through Jack London's prose this time, that stirs its wings only in solitude and stillness, when the empty land brims over with mystery—snowy mountains blue with forest, slickrock canyons gathering shadows, coastal headlands ranging one past another into mist. What excites me in those moments is not a sense of oneness with the land, or even a kinship with it, but more the reverse. I sense the land as something so other, so anciently complete, that my presence makes not a twig of difference. That perception is likely to be very demoralizing or very uplifting. For me it's the latter. In the open land I sense a wholeness that makes my own less-than-wholeness seem unimportant.

I can't say I took in much of the academic wealth Reed College offered. I was ambushed by a different kind of learning, a new curriculum that imposed its own exacting courses and examinations. I arrived in Oregon not long after the arrival of LSD, and before my college career was two months old I was taking it occasionally. Many questions, such as the nature of consciousness and matter, were thrown wide open. More personally, LSD showed me with the subtlety of a sledgehammer that I scarcely had a clue who had been walking around inside my skin for eighteen years. Suddenly I was exposed—to the world, it felt like, but probably only to myself—as a welter of insubstantial identities. Whatever I had been wouldn't do anymore. I was struggling to locate something still and certain I could call myself.

Conversation was difficult when I was tripping, even when I was only stoned on grass. Whatever I said, whatever anybody said, I observed and fretted over. Did it mean this, or—*that?* Did it mean anything? And why was so-and-so laughing now? Why was I laughing? And what exactly did Mick Jagger mean, singing, at the moment, *Goooood-bye, Ruuuuuby Tuesday* . . . ? And now somebody else was saying something, or had said something and I had half-caught it, and I was tangled in self-consciousness like Laocoön with the serpents.

It was outdoors, alone or with one friend at a time, that I could sometimes escape my obsessive self-observation into moments of grace. Once at the coast I ate some psilocybin mushrooms—I found I did better with the milder, organic psychedelics—and walked the beach, experiencing at first only an acute mind-altering headache. But then I noticed how bright and vast and windy the space around me seemed, how the veering and crying seagulls were such . . . *seagulls,* and after a while I found myself gazing a long time at anemones lining the bottom of a tidepool, seeing them look like sunflowers like vaginas like medusa heads like radiant starbursts, and then I was traversing out along the side of a tree-plumed sea stack that had become a low-tide isthmus, thanking the barnacles for giving grip to my boots, laughing at myself for talking to barnacles, and laughing for the pure pleasure of being alive and aware and aflow in the world.

There was a dark section of the traverse, a shadowed seaweedy cleft where I shivered, not quite sure what to do and thinking I should go back. But my hands and feet knew what to do. They took me up a short steep climb into the sudden smack of wind and sun on my face and what I hadn't known I'd been seeking—the sea, the open spangled sea before me, alive with slow combing surges that seemed to move within me as they moved without, foaming on a rock shelf below, pouring back, gathering to surge again. I sat and cried without crying, laughed without laughing. It was as though I had never seen the ocean before, and as though I had known it always for the field of incandescent energy it was. *This is the way it is,* I told myself. *Don't forget. Don't forget.*

And I didn't, but to do more than remember, to live that grace again, always required mushrooms or mescaline or LSD again. "Trip" was the natural expression for what I and many young people in the 60s were doing with psychedelics, but in a way it was exactly wrong. To experience our vision, true and beautiful as it may have been, we undertook no authentic journey. We paid a few bucks for a ticket and waited for the enlightenment show to begin, then waited for it to end—hoped like hell it *would* end—when enlightenment became disturbing or scary. If we were travelers at all we were day-trippers, tourists of the visionary world.

Not every vision was profound. One spring day my friend Danny and I, mellow on mild doses of acid, were lazing under a tree on the Reed lawn. I was sitting, Danny was stretched out on the grass, each absorbed in our own psychedelic proceedings. Birds were singing in the tree. I was in an expansive humor, as if the bright and breezy spring afternoon was the very weather of my being. *This* is the life, I kept thinking, as if pondering a thought of significant weight. The breeze stirred. I thought I felt a light impact on the top of my head. My right hand started to reach up, then stopped halfway. Oh no, I thought. A bird just crapped on my head.

Of course not, I assured myself, lowering my hand. I've never been crapped on by a bird. Why would it happen now, of all times, when I'm on acid?

But maybe it *had* happened. What should I do? My sunny composure had disintegrated. From the side of one eye I glanced at Danny, who was lying on his back gazing up into the tree. He knows, I thought. He's pretending he doesn't, but he does. I started to reach up again and stopped.

My head felt fine. I would know if there was bird crap on my head.

But what if I *didn't* know, and there was? What if I walked around campus and everyone saw it? My trip had gone terribly wrong. Somehow I had to save myself.

"Do you . . . hear the birds?" I heard myself asking.

Danny slowly rolled his head my way. "Those birds know how to sing," he said. He looked up at me, a delighted grin on his face.

He *does* know, I thought. Suddenly my hair felt wet. I started to smell bad smells.

"Yeah," I said. "Um . . . this has never happened before."

"What's never happened? The birds?"

"Well yeah . . . I've never been crapped on by a bird before." I spoke very clearly. It seemed important to make my friend understand.

His face slowly buckled into an enormous laugh, as if I had said the funniest thing in history. "A bird didn't crap on you," he said. "Why do you think a bird crapped on you?"

"Oh, I don't, really," I said. I reached my right hand to the top of my head. As my fingers pressed lightly on my bushy hair I thought they felt something liquid. No, I thought. Sensations get messed up when you're on acid. I lowered my hand. Two fingertips were white, with a subtle shading of purple.

Danny gaped. "Holy moly," he said. "That's an *amazing* color."

It will not surprise you to learn that I washed out of Reed after three semesters. I felt as though none of the reasons I was there were my own, but other people's—my parents', my aunts', my high school teachers'—and my chronic confusions about what I wanted to do or be had reduced me to poor academic material. Psychedelic drugs had intensified my confusion and confirmed my growing (and convenient) belief in the hollowness of book learning. The menu was tasting dry and savorless. I wanted out.

After kicking around back East I settled in San Francisco for a year, thus keeping my promise to the Golden Gate Bridge, then drifted back to Portland in 1969 and fell in with a loose confederacy of rock climbers and mountaineers at Reed. Some were students, some dropouts like me. I liked their learnedly outlaw spirit. I tagged along on rock climbs in the Columbia Gorge, cleaning pitches behind the leaders, learning at the safe end of the rope a feel for vertical movement and for the unreliable character of Oregon's volcanic rock. A favorite playground was Horsethief Buttes, east of the gorge on the Washington side. There we would boulder and do short top-roped climbs in the afternoon heat, wandering the buttes wherever our hands and feet led us. In the evening we rested, cooked a pot of stew on a campfire, passed joints and gallon wine bottles between us, and drifted off to boulder again by moonlight and sit for a while on the butte tops, watching lit tugs and barges passing below on the broad and shining Columbia.

Mount Hood was my first peak. Two friends and I slept a couple of hours in the car and set out from Timberline Lodge at three or so in the morning, our boots and ice axes crunching in the crusted snow. Our slow and steady rhythm mesmerized me, made me feel part of some ancient quest. This was not the Blue Ridge of northern Virginia. Fat stars and planets were glowing as I had never seen them in a gulf of space that expanded as we trekked higher, the dark countryside spreading wide below with its specks and clusters of human light. At some point I shouted for pure joy, scaring hell out of my friend Jackson, who was leading. Above Illumination Rock we stopped to drink water and eat a bite. I noticed a tiny dark motion on the snow. Leaning down, shaking from the cold, I saw a spider—of all creatures!—trucking steadily up the icy grade.

"What are you doing here?" I asked.

"What am *I* doing here?" I answered and broke up in shivery laughter. One small spider and three small humans all wildly out of place on a frozen mountain, out of our minds, maybe—and doing exactly, it seemed to me, what we'd been born to do. The sovereign radiance of dawn was lighting an expansive, ungraspable wholeness within me and without, a cosmos lit with possibility. The spider never stopped climbing, and after a while the rest of us followed.

Climbing is an instinctive desire. Pre-toddlers pull themselves upright before they walk, and soon they climb stairs, furniture, parents, and eventually trees, fitting hands to limbs much as our long-gone ancestors did many millions of years ago in the forests of Africa. To climb rocks and mountains is to be that child, with larger ambitions. But for me it was also, I see now, an escape—from the mess of my parents' marriage, from questions of direction and purpose I couldn't answer, from fears and confusions about personal relationships that I scarcely understood. On cliffs and steep snowfields, usually alone, I knew exactly what I feared. I welcomed the simplifying lens of danger, the way it forced me to focus everything I had on each slight nub or depression in a rock face, to feel the stone's crystalline texture with my fingertips, to stare, momentarily spellbound between moves, at a nest of tiny yellow flowers in a crack six inches in front of my face.

Those flowers were more beautiful than flowers in a garden, and the same was true of birds and clouds and sunsets. The things of the wild flared full of being when they revealed themselves in the course of a climb, most vivid when I was most scared or exhausted. It was like taking a drug but this way earning the payoff, body and mind and spirit working hard in concert to achieve it. If climbing was an escape, it was also a seeking. For several years I pursued it with hunger, far more hunger than skill, as if peaks and clouds and glacial brilliance were symbols of some secret meaning I was forever on the verge of understanding. Mountains, to me, were monuments of nature's joy. I wanted to feel for myself, *in* myself, that elemental joy. In the wild hills if anywhere, I sensed, I might discover the sure and undivided self I longed to be.

There were moments when I found it. The most satisfying climb I made was Mount Olympus, the highest peak in Washington's Olympic Range. I hiked the twenty-mile Hoh River trail, from its start in a mossy rainforest of colossal Sitka spruces up through thinning forests shot through with quick little streams. Now and then I glimpsed a craggy skyline, a bright snowfield of the alpine interior. I took two days, not pushing it, as if the approach to Olympus was a purgatory I needed to make myself worthy of the mountain. And then I broke out of trees into the mountain's presence, almost too bright to behold. I crossed Blue Glacier with its odd whining noises, kicked steps up and over the Snow Dome, and at last dropped my ice axe and climbed the bare summit pinnacle, where I took off my boots and lay cradled in warm stone as windy vapors gathered and dispersed, obscuring and revealing the maze of knifey, white-flanked ridges around me. I had found the center of the world. I lay still as stone, wanting nothing that was not there.

I played in the mountains, and I also worked in the mountains. For parts of two years I set chokers in the southern Washington Cascades for the Weyerhaeuser Timber Company, helping them strip the trees from their forest empire. The timber industry was booming then. Anyone with a half-sound body, even a college dropout with wild hair and wire-rimmed glasses, could go to the Weyerhaeuser office in Longview and be at work in the woods the next morning. It paid $3.32 an hour, a pretty good wage. I hired on with a few other Reed dropouts in the winter of 1969.

Logging is a kind of fishing. The rod is a hundred-foot steel tower, the reel a blasting diesel yarder at the tower's base. The line is heavy steel cable, hundreds of yards long, that runs from the tower down a hill where every tree has been felled and bucked into thirty- or forty-foot lengths. This cable threads through a pulley block hung on a stump, then across the hill, through another block, and back up the hill to the tower and yarder, forming a continuous length arrayed in a triangle. The chokers, hung like fishing leaders on the main line, are two steel cables designed to noose around logs. The yarder operator runs the chokers down the hill. You drag your choker through the jumbled wreckage of forest, wrestle and coax it around the log the rigging slinger has assigned you, and scramble out of the way. The slinger hits his whistle, the yarder roars on the landing, the chokers cinch, and two hemlock or Douglas fir logs start stubbornly up the hill, bucking and flailing, scattering root wads and other logs, plowing long raw trenches in the sodden ground. The chaser on the landing unhooks the logs, the empty chokers come back, and you do it again, and again, and again. You scrabble and stumble, you grub face down in the mud with your choker, you slip on a buckskinned log and fall on your ass, you get whipsawed in the face by a springy fir branch, you stand between turns in the cold rain, smoking a cigarette for warmth and trying hard not to ask what time it is, and all you want is to go home and lie in the tub and not even that, just lie right there in the brush and to hell with the goddamn chokers.

It's the violence that saves it. Grown and not-so-grown men are taken back in the hills and given, with pay, a toy of the size and raw power that kids rolling rocks down a hillside can only dream of. . . . *Jesus stump-fuckin' Christ, look at that son of a bitch go!* old Studhorse the hook tender would shout, dancing on a stump and waving his tin hat as an outsized granddaddy butt-cut eight feet through started up the hill, the cables taut and jumping, singing under the strain. It was exciting, despite my wet weariness and mutterings to myself about ignorant people doing ignorant work and me being ignorant enough to do it with them.

Studhorse and the rest of the crew had seen college kids come and go. They viewed them pretty much as they viewed foreign cars—unreliable, incapable of heavy work, and just all around uncomfortably different.

"Why'd you leave that school?" Stud wanted to know one morning.

"I didn't know what I was doing there," I answered, as honestly as I could.

Stud spat a glob of tobacco juice. "Don't know what you're doin' here neither, I reckon."

I didn't, but I worked with a doggedness that eventually won me a measure of their respect and a measure of my own. It felt good, when four o'clock came, to slouch nearly asleep in the bouncing crummie, thinking of nothing, immersed in the sharp smells of pitch and sweat and the easy banter that swirled around me. The older men had worked in the woods for thirty years or more, and many of the younger ones would work that long before they were done. I scorned what I saw as their simplicity, but I envied their spirit. Despite the tough and dangerous work they did, or maybe because of it, they seemed to wear their lives more comfortably than I wore mine. For the first time I was among people who lived not in cities or suburbs but closer to the land, who split cedar shakes and cut their own cordwood, who hunted and fished and knew their way in the hills. To them, climbing mountains was about as silly as studying philosophy. They were competent to make practical use of nature, not just to play in it. Their speech was placed speech. They were at home in the countryside their families had been part of, in some cases, for three generations or more.

Every morning and evening as the crummies traveled the muddy back roads, I saw the scars of old clearcuts, some replanted with bright young seedlings, but others—many others—growing only thickets of brush around enormous graying stumps. The fresher cuts were nothing but stumps and raw dirt, a litter of branches and splintered wood chunks. I'd like to say that the obvious injury being done to those hills outraged me, or at least made me uncomfortable, but in fact I felt only twinges of concern. When I thought about it at all I rationalized that the Weyerhaeuser Timber Company had the right to use or misuse its property exactly as it damn well pleased—and besides, we all needed wood and paper. I felt no responsibility. Those Washington hills were only the setting of my personal adventure. I had escaped the eastern suburbs, flown the coop of my education, and now was wearing red suspenders and a tin hard hat, chewing tobacco and learning how to cuss from the greatest teachers in the world, tasting what I mythologized as the authentic life of the great Northwest. It wasn't so good in the freezing rain, but Friday evenings behind a steak dinner and many tall pitchers of beer with my friends, it tasted fine.

At some point after coming west I began to see the work of Gary Snyder—a broadside here, a chapbook there, then his *Riprap and Cold Mountain Poems*. The Buddhist references meant little to me, but I felt a strong affinity for the poems. Here was a man who had hitchhiked the West Coast, worked on ocean tankers and in fire lookouts, hiked and climbed and been a logger, and he wrote about those very things, wrote tightly focused poems in which moonlit ridges gleamed, rattlesnakes buzzed, and "All the junk that goes with being human / Drops away . . ." I eagerly imagined Snyder as a dropout like me, little knowing how deeply engaged he was in the life of books and ideas I thought he had repudiated for the life of nature. (At Reed I had never looked up his senior thesis in anthropology, class of 1951.) I really didn't know who or what I was reading in Gary Snyder— I saw him through the haze of my own juvenility. But the poems were compact and tough, their broken lines glinting like bright granite, and they planted in my head and heart the possibility that literature could be made from the present and the immediate, from the very things that I was seeing and the very kind of life that I was living.

I took something of a similar message, though delivered in a very different tone and style, from Wallace Stegner's "Wilderness Letter," which I happened upon in a Sierra Club book. Reading it made me think of my father's impassioned oratory in the union cause, the way he stood up and spoke boldly for what he believed in. Stegner was doing that for western wilderness, in ringing sentences, with measured but intense feeling, with both gravity and a lively spirit. Through him I understood for the first time that the landscapes I was exulting in had significance beyond their service as recreational playgrounds for such as me. Wilderness had human value even if we never set foot in it. It had shaped our history, our American character, and if we let it be destroyed we would lose one of the deep springs of our vitality and hope.

I had long been drawn to the outdoors, and I had

long been drawn to books and learning. I loved both, but the two had seemed almost entirely separate. Stegner and Snyder, in their very unlike ways, showed me that the two could be one.

But they were authors, accomplished and much acclaimed. What was I? A few teachers along the way had encouraged me to write. I loved the *idea* of writing, and by the time I graduated from high school I had developed a romantic self-image as an American author-to-be. I scrawled windy letters to friends and girlfriends, citing passages from Thomas Wolfe and Ernest Hemingway as the kind of literary art I desperately longed to create. But letters, and papers for school, were all I actually wrote. After I dropped out of Reed it was always in the back of my mind that maybe I could write, maybe I would write, but the few times I tried to set down a few words I quickly broke off in disgust. My experiences seemed paltry, unconnected. What did I have to say?

My adventures with psychedelic drugs had contributed to my wordless and feckless condition. The worst experiences, harrowing and seemingly interminable bouts of identity meltdown, were too frightening and confusing to want to express, and the best were ineffable. If, as the *Tao Te Ching* taught, the way that can be told is not the true Way, if the name that can be named is not the eternal Name, then what could be written that was not either a lie or a lesser truth? What was language but a falsification of the experience of true being, or at best, if not a falsification, a measly menu for the Meal?

I wanted to write about climbing, what it felt like, what it meant to me, but I didn't know where to begin.

I told myself I hadn't climbed enough yet, hadn't lived enough. In fact I had plenty to write about, and a need to write it, but not yet the inner means to compose it. To write requires a sense of self, part ego but not ego alone, a gravitational center around which one's memories and imaginings can begin to constellate—and there needs to be a desire from within to look, to explore, to seek and further shape the constellating forms. I had the inchoate desire but not yet the center. Epiphanies on mountaintops, or on drugs, had not been enough to evolve it.

A young man is a dangerous thing, says a friend of mine who once was one. Being a young man of good breeding and some manners, I directed against myself most of the danger I generated. I rode a motorcycle, a BSA Lightning, despite ditching it in a Portlander's begonia bed the first time I mounted it and ditching it several times thereafter. I liked the power, the rush of air, just as I liked the powerful rush of methamphetamine when it hit my system. No longer was I taking drugs for anything as nuanced as personal insight or spiritual vision. I wanted euphoria. I wanted to feel *right*. I was out in the world, but the world was not confirming me. I lived with friends in San Francisco, worked at various jobs, dabbled in Zen meditation, protested the draft and the Vietnam War, joined encounter groups, took sporadic college courses and more drugs. Nothing I did seemed to lead anywhere or to fit with anything else—a ramshackle life, and it was not at all clear who was living it.

The recurrent thread, the authentic trail I kept losing and finding again, was climbing. I bought a rack of pitons and rode my motorcycle to Yosemite, where I hung around Camp Four, the climbers' camp, long enough to work up my courage and ask a veteran if he needed a partner that morning. It happened that he did, and so he and eventually others led me onto the bright granite faces. I reveled in the rock's speckled polish, its tiny fingerholds and clean jam cracks, its rich flinty smell in sun warmth, its arched and pinnacled music always rising. I learned technique, pushed myself, began to lead some pitches and scrape up against my limits as a rock climber. I watched others making moves I couldn't do and envied them, but more than their climbing prowess I envied how they were with themselves, how some of them, only a few years older than me, had an ease about them, a fluid and deliberate way, a habit of being in no hurry and sure in every move.

I met a guy of about my own ability, a chemistry grad student at Cal, and we put ourselves to work on weekends practicing for a big wall. We chose the Chouinard-Herbert route on Sentinel Rock, a 1700-foot line that climbers now scamper up in a few hours. In our primitive era, it was usually done in two days. Early one July morning in 1972, Ted and I scrambled up the brushy scree slope and easy fourth-class pitches, then hit the first roped pitch on the wall itself just as the sun hit us. We weren't bad, we discovered, but we were slow. Wall climbing, as then practiced, was cumbersome. One man led, climbing free where he could, standing in slings where he couldn't, pounding pitons into cracks up the hot vertical granite to a ledge or maybe just a place to hang. He secured himself, drank a quart of water wishing it were a gallon, and went to work raising the haul bag—the climber's equivalent of a steamer trunk—as his partner followed the pitch on a fixed rope, recovering the hardware. Then the partner leapfrogged ahead, at the same plodding pace, up the next pitch. It was an exercise in vertical freight hauling, a laborious raising of bodily mass and the mass of stuff that bodies must have to sustain themselves through two scorching days of hauling mass.

All day we'd been hearing snatches of speech and laughter floating down from a climbing party somewhere on the upper wall. Now came a shout. Something dark was dropping fast out of the brilliance of stone and sky, ripping the air with the sound of an erratic helicopter prop as I crammed myself against the face. The thing had hit the slope five hundred feet down and burst into pieces before I registered what it had been—a pack or a haul bag, crammed full.

"I thought it was a body," said Ted when he reached my belay ledge.

"I did too," I said.

Climbing is a spell, strenuously cast. Rope and hardware, hands and feet, simple will. If the spell breaks, there's only gravity.

It was dusk when we finished the last pitch to the bivouac ledge, which was big enough for two to semi-stretch out and smelled of human shit. Not that we cared. We spent the evening each drinking water and watching the other drink water. Watching like hawks.

"Better save the rest for tomorrow," Ted observed, finishing a long glug.

"Right," I agreed. "We'll need it." I reached for one of the last few quarts and drank half of it. Ted drank the rest of his bottle. We might as well have been discussing foreign policy.

We ate everything in the haul bag that contained a drop of moisture—oranges, a can of corn, a memorable warm cucumber that we snatched from each other's grasp and devoured in big chomps. A thousand feet below, a few lights of sanity moved on the valley floor.

We awoke to pale dawn, the smell of sewage, and the need to move on. Our last swig of water was gone by midmorning. The climbing wasn't especially tough, but the afternoon was a cauldron. We knew it was dumb time, mistake time. We reminded each other to concentrate, to tie the knots right, to place plenty of protection. The last hard pitch was a bulging overhang of semidetached slabs dubbed the Afro-Cuban Flakes by Chouinard and Herbert, far better climbers than we, who had evidently had the time and good humor—and the water—to pause during their first ascent to draw music from the slabs with their hammers. The pitch seemed to take us hours and probably did. As Ted made the lead I watched inner-tubers float the Merced River in the green valley a quarter of a mile beneath me. When he reached the belay point I followed on the fixed rope, swinging wildly over the void as I carelessly unclipped the rope from one after another of the expansion bolts the first ascenders had pounded in to surmount the overhang.

Ted was belaying from a huge ledge. Above, it looked like easy ledge scrambling to the top. The sun was down. We decided to rest briefly, then climb up and over the top and down the easy gully behind Sentinel until we came to water. It would be dark, but we had a flashlight.

An hour later we were still sitting. Moving had turned out to be unlikely. We ate what we could get down without water and fell asleep where we were. My tongue felt huge, my mouth dry as the granite I lay on. Slow, fluent colors, vivid reds and purples, moved through me all night, not dreams exactly but a kind of hallucinatory tide. I felt empty, weightless. Ted's voice called me to daylight. We packed quickly and clambered up the easy ledges. At the top of Sentinel stood a solitary ponderosa pine, its bark a vibrant orange with black furrows, tigerish, its crown of boughs shot with sun. The tree glowed, seethed in my vision, as if it could not contain its own bright being. As Ted went ahead I stumbled to the pine and pressed my forehead to its trunk, breathing its hot vanillic aura. I took a flake of bark shaped like a puzzle piece.

We slid and scrambled down the dry gully, telling each other to slow down and be careful as we both slid faster, slipping and scraping ourselves, breathing mouthfuls of dust. Where the gully opened onto the scree slope, a little stream flowed through grass and shrubs and horsetails so green they hurt my eyes. We dumped our packs and knelt in the stream and lifted spilling handfuls to our mouths. It burned like cold fire inside me. My heart skittered, beat double a few times, settled to a steady boom. We wet our hair, rubbed the grime from our hands and faces, laughed, chattered like children. The stream flowed from its high hidden springs, lively, clear, unmeasured, and free.

As I've written in an essay called "The Impoverishment of Sightseeing," I returned to Yosemite Valley in the

1980s with my wife and mother and was surprised how inert and ordinary the valley walls looked through the frame of a tour bus window. Half Dome, Sentinel, El Capitan, all seemed mere visual objects, scenes. My experience of one of the great natural spectacles of the world felt rote and passionless, and I thought I saw the same disconnection in the other tourists that day. Their pleasure in the beauty around them seemed muted, as if, though drawn to nature, they remained somehow insensible to it. As I and the rest of us clicked our photos and showed the valley to our video cameras, it felt as though we were trying to verify that what we saw was actually there and that we were actually seeing it.

In our contemporary world we have split off visual beauty from the greater experience of nature, and in doing so we have forfeited a beauty far more lively and robust. To know that greater beauty requires the exercise of more than the eyes, and it can't be done at a distance. It takes time, sweat, and sometimes pain, a willingness to enter the land and engage it. Backpackers, birders, hunters, fishers, climbers, surfers, river runners, tree sitters, homesteaders, field scientists, small farmers, small ranchers, and backwoods lunatics are more likely to know this beauty than are those who only stop their cars at the scenic vistas. They won't automatically know it—there are climbers who care only about bagging peaks, birders keener on lists than on birds, ranchers to whom grass is little more than poundage of beef—but the fullness of natural beauty is potentially available to them. They have the opportunity to become part, for a time, of places that onlookers can only observe.

As I was climbing and hiking and drifting in the

early 70s I was reading conservation magazines, developing a rudimentary awareness of western environmental issues, the principles of ecology. I was beginning to understand nature conceptually as a living system that places limits on us even as it sustains us. But such understanding is wan and forceless unless we learn it through the body and senses as well as the intellect. The first axiom of ecological awareness, it seems to me, is that the universe does not exist for human convenience and does not especially care if human life, individual or collective, continues or comes to an end. This can't be well understood as a purely abstract proposition. It was the Blue Ridge rattlesnakes that first brought it home to me, and further experiences have ratified the lesson— the humbling cold along Interstate 5, the heat and the hurtling haul bag on the face of Sentinel Rock, a black bear I watched once in the High Sierra ripping through the contents of my backpack as if she owned them, which she did.

Almost every outing has advanced my ecological education by expanding my sensory imagination. Those thirsty hours in Yosemite's cauldron taught me something my mind only thought it knew—that moisture makes life possible, that its absence sets hard boundaries on where and how and how long life can thrive. Having clambered over fallen old-growth trees in the maritime Northwest and smelled the good dark smells of moss and soil and rotting wood, I better appreciate that a healthy community needs to carefully conserve and recycle its common wealth to sustain itself through time. The word *home* meant something more to me, something I might have learned no other way, when I saw

Chinook salmon three feet long shadowing the small streams of their birth in the Idaho Sawtooths, eight hundred river miles and eight tall dams from their lives in the North Pacific. Feeling a twenty-five pounder thrust doggedly against my line in a coastal Oregon river informed me, too, just as eating his flesh would later inform my body. Even the memory of a night spent in the smell of human excrement recurs to me with vivid, if depressing, connections. I think of it when I'm stuck in traffic and the odor of mingled exhaust fumes seeps into my car, and when I drink city tap water that tastes as though it's been drawn from a swimming pool.

But most of what I've learned from my outings, like the language I've absorbed, remains unconscious. It contributes to my being in ways I can't analyze or explain, ways I can only feel grateful for. Somehow, after Sentinel and other climbs and backcountry treks, my steps took on a trace more substance. I belonged a little better to my life. For some of us, the way in must first lead out. Because we don't know who we are we must escape ourselves, forget ourselves, bewilder ourselves in a bigger beauty in order to realize, years later, watching breakers pound a headland or a red-tail adrift in the summer sky, that life is not something still ahead or hoped for but what we are living, and that smiling inside us, though we don't always know it or act in ways worthy of it, is that undivided self we had desired but hadn't known how to seek or even to ask for.

LANDSCAPE AND LANGUAGE

I wasn't sure of much in my twenties, but I was sure I belonged in the West. D.C. and the East were home only in that most of my personal history had taken place there and my parents and several good friends lived there. When I went back it was only to visit. Somehow I understood that the riddle of my being was interfused with the western land, with mountains and bright rivers and the shore of the sundown sea.

I kept leaving Oregon for the Bay Area and the Bay Area for Oregon. At twenty-five, as aimless and adrift as ever, I headed north for a railroad job in Klamath Falls, just east of the Cascades and north of the California line. It was a case study in landscape shock. My girl-friend and I, driving past midnight, pulled in to a rest stop on U.S. 97 just short of town. We woke a few hours later to a woeful spectacle under a low gray sky—barren hills and sagebrush flats, dreary in old scraps of snow. A few disconsolate junipers were the only trees. I felt robbed. Where was Oregon? I had been east of the Cascades in earlier years to rock climb, but evidently I had failed to notice, or to care, that the landscape was not wooded and verdantly green. I may have been in love with the West, but I sure didn't know the West.

The job was good, though, demanding only a few hours a day in the railroad yards inspecting the contents of boxcars, and small-town life was good too. Clean air to breathe, a parking place when I needed one, and—most refreshing of all—fewer choices. In San Francisco and Berkeley, every poster on every café window or tele-phone pole, announcing this encounter group or that spiritual teacher or some social cause or a night course in most anything, had tweaked me like a rebuke. People doing those things were finding themselves, I imagined, or already had. I don't know why I gave them such credit, but it was clear to me that they were all getting somewhere. They knew what they were doing.

I hiked and fished and skied in the mountains I had expected to be living in—they weren't far away—and I also began to explore the alien country, the sage and juniper steppeland extending everywhere but west. I found I liked the way junipers apportioned themselves on the rocky slopes. There was something decent, civilized, about the room they granted one another. I liked the way each stocky tree stood whole and solitary in its shaggy bark and dense crown, some of them speckled with constellations of sky blue berries. The basalt scabrock that littered the landscape made walking awkward, but even it had a rough beauty, crusted as it often was with orange and yellow lichen. I remember sitting on a rock one afternoon watching cloud shadows travel the hills, a light breeze stirring the dry bronco grass and the hair on my arms. Something in that spacious stillness seemed to be settling me, easing my confusions. The great dry land was an open secret, and the secret, maybe, had room for me.

Most weekday mornings in the Burlington Northern freight yards, I spent some time talking with the hoboes where they jungled up beneath an overpass, heating cans of food by a fire and frequently passing a bottle of sweet wine. They marveled at my job; I enjoyed their stories. At home I wrote about them, jotting down their adventures, the way they spoke, the kinds of chalk artwork they rendered on the sides of boxcars. (They were tagging before there were taggers.) Eventually I began a short story about two hoboes who find a credit card that turns out to be their undoing. I drafted and redrafted for months, ignoring the little pile of penciled pages for days at a time, then returning to it, swinging between inflated excitement and simple despair at the clear skilllessness of my craft. When I didn't know what to write I held my mouth a different way, and sooner or later I found some sentences. I started another story, a firstperson account of a college dropout who becomes a logger, and worked it over and over with William Sweet, a writer and correspondence-course instructor who lived upstate. He gave me my first lessons on trite language, economy, and narrative movement, and he encouraged me. I began a story about a couple in their twenties on the verge of separating.

My girlfriend and I had endured two years of our own volatile weather in California, and nothing changed in Oregon. Of our several problems, one was central. I loved her, but I wasn't ready yet for the commitment or the emotional intimacy of a long-term relationship. I knew and didn't know that I wasn't ready. I had no clear idea of what I wanted or what I felt about anything, particularly myself. My girlfriend said I was too selfenclosed, I didn't give enough of myself. It was true, but what did I have to give? If I was holding out on her, I was holding out on myself too. We were a breakup waiting to happen, and after a while she stopped waiting. She went to law school in Eugene and fell in love with a professor.

My father died that same year, and, attempting a first

ascent at Castle Crags, I took a leader fall and broke my ankle. Living alone, off work for months as my ankle tried to heal, I turned my losses into language. I took the train to Eugene and bought the biggest dictionary I could find, a *Webster's Third International.* I bought a used Royal manual typewriter and lots of paper and pencils. I wrote observations, sketches, bits of overheard speech in a notebook. I recorded my dreams in another notebook. I wrote a story, my first to be published— sixty bucks—about a climber who breaks his ankle in a fall and broods over a lost girlfriend. I worked hard at a longer story about a native culture in a postnuclear future in which many fewer women than men are born. When a young woman comes of age, the young men ritually climb a mountain by randomly assigned routes. First to the summit gets the girl. My adolescent first-person narrator makes a dramatic ascent but—surprise!— comes in second.

Yet another story about a man dealing with the loss of a woman came back from an editor with the comment, "You write lyrically about landscape." I took his remark as a slam on my story, but over the next few months I began to see what he had seen. I was relieved and cheered when I did. I hadn't known it, but I was sicker than hell of rewriting my tale of lovelorn youth. I realized, vaguely at first, that I wrote lyrically about landscape because I *felt* lyrically about landscape, about the very landscape I was living in, that had shocked me with its bleak aridity when I first saw it. I came to understand that I didn't want to create human worlds out of words. I wanted to touch with words, to articulate as best I could, the beauties and mysteries of the natural world around me.

And so my fiction died, and poems sprouted in its place. I quit my railroad job—I'd felt guilty for some time about using it as a climbing, writing, and advanced beer drinking fellowship—and moved east out of town to a ranch in Langell Valley owned by a family I had just met. I rented a small crumbling house for fifty dollars a month and shared it with a freeloading pack rat. I didn't know how to write poems, real poems, but I had read some—Frost and Jeffers mainly, some Roethke, Rexroth, Snyder and the other Beats—and I knew how those poems sounded, what they looked like on the page. I knew how certain ones moved me. I wanted my poems to do that. I wrote about sandhill cranes and great horned owls, about the smell of sagebrush after a thunderstorm, about rimrocks and canyons, about the yip and wail of coyotes in starry darkness, about splitting firewood and pulling a calf and climbing a tall ponderosa pine with one of my friends' kids.

It turned out that climbing, like fishing before it, had in a way prepared me for creative writing. The emotional terrain was similar. I knew what it was to labor in tense uncertainty, hoping that one move would lead to the next. I knew it was sometimes necessary to go a way I hadn't seen at the start. I knew what it was to press myself on by sheer grit. I knew what it was to fail and try again. And I knew the exhilaration and good fatigue that came with the completion of a long and difficult effort, beginning to middle to end, and the reward of seeing a little more in the end than I had seen in the beginning.

In 1979 William Stafford came down to teach at a Klamath Falls writing conference. His poems, as he read them aloud and later as I read them on the page, seemed to create around themselves an intense cumulative quiet, an aura of possibility. They weren't *rhetoric,* I realized, thinking painfully of my own work in contrast. The poems made no claims but simply opened like flowers— or didn't open, but even the ones that stayed obscure to me glinted with hidden life, like fish in deep water. They called forth an alertness, a generosity of attention, by offering the same. In "Vocation," one of the poems Stafford read, his father says to Stafford's boy-self, "Your job is to find what the world is trying to be." That was the poet's work, I decided. That job would be worth all the years and concentration I could possibly put into it.

William Stafford's reading at the conference was my first exposure to the view of creative writing he preached, gently and nimbly and insistently, in all his readings and writings about poetry. Anyone who breathes is in the rhythm business, he liked to say, and anyone who speaks is engaged with language. A creative writer is one who gives sustained attention to the promptings of language and is willing to follow where they lead. Often they lead nowhere, but sometimes they take you to a wholeness, a crystallization of sense and sound that would never have occurred if you hadn't trusted your blind and tentative initial jottings. That wholeness may be a poem. If it's a bad poem, good. You've got it out— now you can make yourself available to what's next. The well is deep, and unless you start telling it what it ought to yield, it's inexhaustible.

That was hopeful and helpful news to a young

man—if thirty-one is young—writing what he hoped were worthy poems. A few weeks after the conference I emboldened myself and sent William Stafford a few of my efforts, asking if he could recommend me to the state arts commission for a job as a poet in the schools. He could, he wrote back, noting which of the poems he liked best and what he found appealing about them without making more of them than they deserved. He told me what he told countless other new writers first trying themselves out. "Trust yourself. Keep writing." I did, and over the years I found Stafford the man to be as thoroughly honest, stalwart, and generous as his poems. Whenever our acquaintance brought us together I felt realigned with the authentic.

The ranch was the first place I lived where stepping out-doors meant something more than leaving the house. It meant *space,* no crowd of other houses, a lot of sky be-tween the horizons. Beyond the ponderosa pine grove east of the house, a rim dotted with junipers ran south to north and curled northwest, edging a pine-covered plateau that was national forest land. To the south was open pasture, sagebrush flat, and the gorge of Miller Creek canyon. To the west, a gradual rise of juniper woodland, and in the distance, the long blue spine of Bryant Mountain. Another mountain, Yainax Butte, stood far to the northwest. It was a landscape both open and comfortably enclosing. Cows and sheep and horses were the most evident forms of four-legged life, but there also were deer, occasional pronghorns, a coyote if you were lucky. And there was silence. Or rather, many silences—silence of wind in the pine tops, of the hawk's harsh whistle, of before thunder and after, of hooves hitting dusty ground, of sprinklers whispering in fields of hay, of cattle lowing, owls calling, snowfall drifting from a February sky.

My backpacking rambles had taken me into such silences, but in those I had been a brief visitor. Here I was living in silence, at home in it, in ongoing league with it except on certain occasions when Beethoven or the Rolling Stones insisted they be heard by pines and owls and rimrock. Becoming aware of the gift of silence was like slowly realizing I'd had a headache for most of my life, and now it was going away. Like so much else in our natural lives, we have forfeited silence by small gradations, scarcely aware of the thickening calluses that cover our day-to-day hearing, disconcerted and even frightened when moments of full quiet overtake us. The same with darkness. Any clear night at the ranch, I could walk out to true dark and the specked and studded brilliance of the Milky Way. Our species was born and came of age in that nightly presence. We saw the stars and somehow came to be aware that we were seeing them, came to fear, to hope, to wonder. And now we wander in the obliterating glare of our own lights, the beeping and bellowing din of our human noise, lost—happily or wretchedly, but lost—in what we have made, progressively deafened and blinded to that which made us.

In winter my favorite indoor light was the one that shone through the translucent mica screen of the wood stove—or, as it titled itself, the Parlor Furnace. It put out blasting heat when stoked but didn't damp down well enough to hold a fire through the night, and so sometimes I woke to a twenty-five-degree room and the perplexity of wanting and not wanting to do something about it. Doing something sooner or later won out, and when it did I took pleasure, even as my teeth rattled in my head, in huddling close to the Parlor Furnace to absorb its first wan radiance, knowing that more was on the way. I had invested some work in that warmth. With my friends I had felled pine snags in the national forest, trucked them home in sections, split the sections in my driveway, stacked the fragrant split pieces in the covered porch of my house and resplit some for kindling, and carried in enough the night before to get a quick fire going in the morning. My life was far from self-sufficient—I didn't build my house or raise my own food or generate my power—but in the way of winter warmth I had provided one essential need, and I took satisfaction in that.

As I lived and wrote through the seasons of four years at the ranch, I began to know it and the country around it as a home I might somehow belong to, though none of it belonged to me. For some time I had felt I belonged to the American West, and to the Northwest especially, but that was a generalized allegiance. There were specific wilderness places where I felt I belonged, but that was the belonging of a guest or perhaps a pilgrim, not that of a resident. Through my reading of Aldo Leopold and others I was beginning to understand that humankind was a member, and needed to act like a member, of the greater natural community, but that was a conceptual formulation. At the ranch for the first time I *felt* I belonged to a particular landscape, and it was Wendell Berry, writing of a very different terrain, who helped me imagine what I felt. In one of his poems in

The Country of Marriage he likened himself to a dying elm tree near his home on the Kentucky River. Both his and the elm's, he wrote, were lives he knew the country by. Both drew their strength from their place and would fall in that place, both were "timely and at home, neighborly as two men." I recognized in those lines, and throughout Berry's poems, an intimacy and interdependence I had hungered for without knowing it.

I knew I could never realize in myself the full measure of his belonging—I was short half a lifetime and several ancestral generations in my place—but whatever portion of belonging could be mine, I wanted. I saw how disconnectedly I had shuttled across the surface of the American land. The ranch with its surroundings was the first landscape I stayed in long enough to see and to come to love. I would eventually shuttle on from there too, and when I did, for the first time in my life it hurt to leave not just friends and family, but a place as well.

As felt as my sense of belonging may have been, however, it was a bit shallow when it came to responsibility. For most of one year, when food stamps and hauling mortar for a mason friend and working as a poet in the schools weren't enough to get me by, I entered the firewood business. I enjoyed the work—it brought back some of the rough joy of my logging days—so why not make a little money at it? I drove the back roads on top of the rim, scouting for the sere needles of pines not long deceased. I got to be good enough with a chainsaw to drop the chosen snag generally where I wanted it to go, or at least not to drop it where I really didn't want it to go. (My standards weren't then and aren't now very high. In the falling of a sizable tree, success is not falling it on yourself.) One pine of seventy or eighty feet, bucked up into sixteen-inch sections, yielded three groaning loads in my little pickup, loads that squashed the rear tires nearly flat and caused the front of the truck to weave weightlessly side to side as I drove home.

On days I didn't fall timber, I put on wood-splitting music—Beethoven's Ninth was best, though John Fahey and Jerry Jeff Walker were good too—and intoxicated with music and the smell of pitch, I swung my sledge and maul like some John Henry of the pine woods, the heaps of bright split pieces rising around my chopping block like an ode to joy. I sold five cords to a rancher down the road, delivered and stacked, and stacked fairly, too, much more wood than air. Thirty-five dollars a cord. A friend in town bought three cords, someone else ordered two. It was turning into a booming little industry, and a pleasant one, except for the hours of brain-curdling chainsaw screech.

It all came to a whimpering halt one afternoon when a man pulled up in a pickup where I was bucking up the latest pine I'd laid low. Uh-oh, I thought. The truck was civilian, but the man was walking toward me with a Forest Service stride.

"What the hell do you think you're doing?" he wanted to know.

"Well," I started.

"You can't cut firewood here. This is a research natural area. Do you even have a permit?"

"Um," I continued, "do I need one?"

This was disingenuous. I wasn't thoroughly versed in the legalities of firewood cutting on national forest land, but I was aware that officially you were supposed to get a permit and cut only where and what you were told. I had decided that a local guy like me, scratching out a small living by the sweat of his brow on land he supported as a taxpayer, didn't need to fool with a permit.

The man's anger was not just bureaucratic. "I don't have the authority to cite you," he said—the first good news I'd heard—"but I sure as hell would if I could. Do you know how many species of animals use snags like this?"

"No," I answered truthfully, but I was not entirely ignorant of the matter. Though the old-growth wars of the 90s were still a decade away, and information about the ecological role of standing and fallen snags hadn't been much publicized, I was by this time an environmental partisan, a proponent of expanded wilderness protections, an enemy of rampant logging. I was reading poems at Greenpeace and Defenders of Wildlife rallies, publishing a few in environmental journals. I knew that my vigorous little entrepreneurship did not entirely square with my felt and written values. I had preferred not to think about the dissonance.

But such clarity came only later. Driving home after the bust I was mad as a Sagebrush Rebel, cussing in my head the officious son of a bitch who had chanced into my private economy—he'd heard the saw and spent half an hour homing in on me—and knocked the bottom out of it. My simmer hit a boil again a couple of hours later when I drove back to the scene of the crime to load up the sections I'd bucked before the law had shown up, only to find that the law had confiscated the evidence. *That'll do the bugs and squirrels a lot of good,* I noted to the silent forest, and drove home empty for the second time that day, my jeans and t-shirt itchy with sawdust and stinking of chainsaw fumes.

I left the ranch in 1982, having won, to my astonishment, a graduate poetry fellowship in Stanford University's creative writing program. In my midthirties, fifteen years after dropping out of college, I finally had a reason to go back. I studied poetry writing in workshops with Kenneth Fields, W. S. Di Piero, and Denise Levertov, and initially audited and then enrolled in my first college-level courses in literature. To be treated as a poet, a term I still wouldn't utter in reference to myself, was a vast validation. I read hungrily, wrote poems and revised them dozens of times, and began to develop a critical sense of what was healthy in my work and what wasn't. The fellowship led to five years of part-time teaching at Stanford, during which I finished an M.A.—without, to my pleasure, first securing a B.A.—and shaped up the manuscript that would become my first book of poems. Those years were an invaluable apprenticeship in the writing and teaching vocations.

Another lucky turn extended the fellowship outside the classroom. When I got the teaching job, I needed a place to live. The creative writing director told me that Wallace and Mary Stegner might have a cottage to rent. They did, and with my wife, Marilyn, whom I married in 1983, I lived in it for five years. The Stegners had settled on their land in the Peninsula foothills above Stanford in 1950, four years after Stegner had joined the Stanford English faculty and founded the creative writing program. Our cottage, just downslope from their house, had been his original writing hut, the place where he had written his "Wilderness Letter." I worked off part of our rent gardening and doing other chores around the property, sometimes alone and sometimes in Wallace Stegner's company. Then in his midseventies, he had retired from Stanford a decade earlier to devote himself to his writing.

I found myself admiring in the man what I admired in his work—his dignified but unstiff manner, his wry humor, his considered optimism, and the immense and varied learning he carried as easily as a gardening trowel. He talked as readily about baseball as he did about Cicero, recited from memory Frost and Wordsworth and bawdy song lyrics from his youth, referred as knowledgeably to medieval Italy as he did to the frontier American West. Devoted both to books and to the natural world, a husband and father as well as a teacher and first-rate writer in several prose genres, he was by far the wholest man I had known. He was also the hardest working. Every morning, early as the birds, the nimble percussion of his Olympia manual typewriter sounded from his study, where he usually stayed holed up until noon. He wrote *Crossing to Safety* in the years we lived on his place. Some afternoons he'd say the novel had moved a little that morning, and he'd get after the job at hand, digging or pruning or constructing a shed, with an extra dash of boyish spirit.

I observed his discipline and tried to stiffen my own. I began to write personal essays in those years, using Wallace Stegner's prose and Henry David Thoreau's as my principal models. I hadn't studied sentences since charting them in junior high school. I studied Stegner's, appreciating their variety and balance, the way he let the long ones run but always under his call. I looked at the way he wove narrative and exposition and grew argument from both, the way passion interfused the argument without softening it, the way he lit serious prose with touches of humor, the way he mustered factual information to the service of his essay but not so much that the writing bogged down. I especially admired his humility. Like the other nature essayists I was reading—Thoreau, Loren Eiseley, Joseph Wood Krutch, Edward Abbey, Wendell Berry—Wallace Stegner called the reader's attention to the worthy and enduring things of the world, both human and transhuman, not to the emotive splendor of his responses to those things, and not to the considerable virtuosity of his own language.

In 1979, living at the ranch, I had sent a few poems to Wendell Berry, asking for his comments. He struck me as the kind of writer who might answer a letter. In a few weeks he did, in longhand on yellow legal paper. He kindly but clearly criticized the poems as too diffuse and prosaic. A poem, he wrote, must enact its own necessity as verse. If it doesn't, why not write it as prose? At Stanford I realized that I was so invested in becoming a poet that I was trying to grow a poem from every seed I happened upon. I had made a few attempts at longer poems but hadn't been able to sustain them. Like many contemporary poets, I was trapped in the one-page lyric. It was a relief to apply Berry's standard and turn some of my energy to the writing of narrative and meditative essays. The process was much the same—seeing something nearsightedly and setting out to see it better, attending to the sounds as well as to the sense of language—but I didn't have to achieve the concentrated focus a poem must realize quickly. Some seeds want a more leisurely gestation and development.

The Stegners, both Wally and Mary, influenced me in another way. I enjoyed and envied their knowledge of and comfort in their place, which they liked to maintain as a semidomesticated wild. Their low, pale green house nestled just below the crest of a hill in a grove of native oaks; one wide-spreading live oak rose through an opening in the deck it shaded. Beds and brick walkways were laid out informally, hedges trimmed in curving lines rather than sharp angles. Wally and Mary held between them nearly four decades of local lore and natural history, some of it a bit fuzzied by time. As I sat in a tree with a pruning saw, awaiting word from the two of them of which branch to lop next, I liked to hear them dispute—always good-naturedly—how old the tree was, whose idea it had been to plant it, what tree or shrub had preceded it, and which of the two of them might have been responsible for an unfortunate pruning job ten or twenty or thirty years in the past.

Once, digging a trench for a septic line from a new bathroom, I unearthed a small midden of bottles and rusted cans and hailed Wally to come look at it. "Kids," he said. "They used to camp here and have their parties before we bought the land." I dug a little farther, turning up a few more bottles and a crumpled California license plate. The year of the plate's issue was stamped into one corner: 1952, two years into the Stegner tenure on the hill. I didn't show it to Wally. I thought, that's what I want. To live long enough in one place to generate my own archaeology, and long enough to interpret it when some kid digs it up.

That evening Marilyn and I drank a bottle of burgundy on the gravel patio behind our cottage. With a toast to the Stegners, I hurled the empty bottle into the hillside field for raccoons to sniff in the dark. Wally and Mary had been about our age, in their late thirties, when they came to Stanford and their place in the hills. Imagining the pleasure they must have taken in their new home added to our own pleasure in living there. We were happy, with the place and with each other. In my twenties I hadn't wanted to marry. I'd been too busy pursuing freedom, which I conceived—or would have, if I'd bothered to think about it—as a state of responsibility to nothing and to no one outside of myself. Doing my own thing, as the 60s mantra had it. It was only after living in eastern Oregon had evoked a longing for place, and after the right woman had come along, that I hungered for a settled relationship. Our culture urges us in countless ways to extend our adolescent freedom, to escape the real or imagined limits imposed by an allegiance to place, spouse, work, and community. In my thirties I began to realize, very vaguely at first, that a steady diet of that freedom is no more sustaining than a candy bar, and that the possibility of true freedom begins not in the simplism of nonattachment but in the complex simplicity of belonging.

WINTER CREEK

We have found that place, the one where we want to put down some archaeology. In 1988, homesick for Oregon, we came back and came to stay. We settled first in Portland, where there was work for us and services for my aging mother, who came from the East to live four years with us. Portland, that good gray city of bridges and bookstores and the best beer in America, an even better city than it had been in the 60s when I first came west. But even in the best cities I feel like a guest at a party. It's entertaining, the company is interesting and usually friendly, but it's loud and busy and it wears me down. I get tired of the hullabaloo. I want to go home.

And so, in 1994, after my mother had died and a job for Marilyn had opened downstate, we bolted to the country. We bought a plain brown box of a house on an acre of trees and creek bottom in the Coast Range foothills west of Eugene. We traded street lights for stars, chlorinated water for our own well, sirens and the snarl of traffic for wind in the trees, the calls of frogs and owls, the seasonal music of a little stream. It took forty-six years and thirty-two dwellings in nine states and the District of Columbia, but I've arrived where I expect to stay.

It could have been somewhere else. Once you're ready to put down roots you can probably put them down in many kinds of soil, but I'm glad to be sinking mine in western Oregon, the region where I first lived when I came west but never really saw. It has its unique generosities. Green the whole year round is one, blackberries and blueberries and raspberries and huckleberries and other berries are another. And trees. The drama of eastern Oregon is in its spacious distances; here the drama sprouts from the soil and grows straight up. The trees on our place, many Douglas firs and one lanky, willful Oregon white oak that managed to keep pace, losing most of its limbs in the process, rise a hundred feet and higher. They lift my gaze whenever I step outside, day or night. In summer they keep the house cool. In the occasional windstorms of fall and winter they sway and creak, shedding dead limbs and live boughs, as Marilyn and I incant spells for the endurance of roots and fiber.

It isn't perfect here. We live near the southern end of the Willamette Valley, which was characterized rapturously to prospective Oregon Trail emigrants as a New Eden. I'd like to know how Edenic it felt after their first winter. It rains here. From mid-October well into June, it rains most days, and the days it doesn't rain, it wants to. Our place crawls with slugs, tree frogs, newts with toxic skin secretions. Mushrooms, some of them poisonous, erupt from the dank ground. Moss overruns the grass of the yard, builds in silent green waves on the roof. Marilyn and I tramp about in slickers and knee boots, muttering, leaving footprints six inches deep. The trees drip, the downspouts gurgle obsessively, the burden of sodden air flattens ferns to the ground. The days drift grayly one to the next, the nights only darker spells of gray.

The stream helps us through. In November, as all else is subsiding into gray slumber, we watch for its return to our surface world from the nether region where it flows in summer. Usually I hear it before I see it. I'll be standing on the deck late at night thinking about something, and suddenly I'll hear what I'd forgotten to listen for— a faint silvery lilt from the darkness below, a hubbub of tiny tongues. As weeks go by and the rains come down the song gets sloshier, accumulates a pouring power. The stream has work to do and goes about it all winter and spring, easing off from time to time, then remembering its business.

Winter Creek, as we call it, sang loudest in February 1996 as heavy rains fell on snow across the Coast Range and the Cascades and flooded the rivers of western Oregon. The creek, which normally I can straddle with my legs, rose out of its banks and swept the bottom of the draw in a turbulent whitewater fan some thirty feet across. Its voice intensified to a shrill steady chant, full of the sounds that inhabit such words as *freshet, surge, hiss.* The previous summer I had raised corn, beans, and potatoes in the bottom, the only part of our acre sunny enough—barely—for the purpose. Now, when the creek returned to its channel, I found the tilled plots wormed with shallow gullies. Small slabs of grassy bank were slumping into the stream. Soil had moved, catastrophically in some places, all across our part of the state, especially where ground had been broken for logging roads and clear-cuts. Nothing catastrophic had occurred on our land, but erosion no longer was somewhere else and attributable to someone else. I had brought it home.

And in that way, the place took up a conversation I had unwittingly begun. I had asked the creek bottom to do something, and it had done it, and now the creek bottom was suggesting that I not ask the same thing again, unless I was ready to cede still more of its soil to the Pacific Ocean. I'm still working on my reply. For now, I'm staying away from crops that require big plots and planting some that don't require annual tilling—raspberries, asparagus, fruit trees. I grow tomatoes and cucumbers in small plots or individual holes. To slow storm flows in our seasonally uninhibited stream, I'm trying out check dams made of small boulders I've hauled in and limbwood from our trees. Marilyn and I are planting native riparian species to help hold the banks as we remove the blackberry brambles that have overrun them.

Sweet corn and pole beans are a powerful lure. To grow things taller than I am *and* good to eat is a vast satisfaction. I may succumb, and if I do, the least I owe my creek bottom is a fall cover crop. But I'm looking beyond our acre, too. Mac and Bonnie, our friends a five-minute walk down the road, have a perfect place for vegetable gardening, a broad, sandy-soiled shelf above the Long Tom River. As we've gotten to know them, they've invited us to share in their summer produce for a consideration of trade or money we work out annually. Corn *wants* to grow in their sunny garden and can without damage to the place. And so the conversation with our creek bottom has taken us a step into our human community as well as into an improved relationship with our land.

I don't want to make more of this conversation than it warrants. My responses have been slow and limited. They are small steps, baby steps, but steps of a kind I haven't taken before. Like most conservationists, I've been quick to blame corporations, government agencies, and large landholders when they have injured what Aldo Leopold called the land community. The small damage I inflicted on my creek bottom in thoughtless conspiracy with the climate persuaded me that all human members of the community, even the best-intentioned, are capable of causing it harm, and that the first condition of our membership must be a reasonable submission to the good of the community over time. Climbing peaks and backpacking in wilderness areas have taught me much, but they didn't teach me that. And nothing could have taught me, I suspect, if I hadn't finally been ready to settle here, or somewhere, for the duration.

The duration, of course, means more—many more, I hope—seven-month winters of rain and gloomy sky. It's good weather for writing, I've found, and it's also good for the cultivation of complaint, which I take to be a privilege of putting down roots. In California I decided that home is the place you stay long enough to begin to see. Now I believe in a tougher standard: home is the place you decide to stay in spite of the miserable weather. And though it seems every year that the clammydamp winter will never end, that the patter of rain on the roof will at last succeed in driving us permanently insane, the day does come when the sun goofs up and shows itself. We stagger, dazzled, groping for eyedrops and dark glasses. We listen for the song sparrow, the whirring of swifts that nest each spring in our chimney. The first trillium opens. A goldfinch flashes. Dogwoods spread a white rumor. Rhododendrons stage their gaudy show. Winter Creek sends off flashing glints and sings a cheerier tune. The green world sparkles.

Eden? No.

But close enough.

At least once a year in spring or summer, we'll be driving a road within five miles of home, a road we know so well we could steer it asleep, and as we round a curve something's different. Light, openness, where trees should be. A patch of forest—an acre, ten acres, twenty— is gone. Left behind is a ground-level strew of green boughs, splintered limbs, rotten or fractured pieces of trunk, gouts of scraped-up soil, and lots of salal and sword fern that would be blinking, if they had eyes, at the torrent of unaccustomed light. Usually a sparse few trees still stand, scrawny Douglas firs—silly looking without their peer group—and maybe an old tree or two well past commercial value. The sharp fragrance of sap hangs in the air.

If not for the trees enclosing our acre, we would see a big fresh clear-cut on a hill to the south and several older ones to the north. The farther hills, the ones we see while driving, sport on their flanks and skylines erratic buzz cuts as weird as anything kids wear to the mall. I sometimes walk a logging road that climbs a ridge not far from home, up through clear-cuts replanted with perky, foot-high seedlings, then through an older cut with ten-foot saplings, and on to the top of the ridge and a patch of standing timber left like a topknot on a mostly shaven head. The trees aren't big, which may explain why they're still upright, except for three mossy veterans. One in particular has candelabra limbs the size of modest trees themselves, the limbs raising an array of branches into a dense crown that somewhere has a top, maybe a hundred-fifty feet up. The veterans weren't always so few. Walking the ridgetop—not where you expect to find the biggest trees—I pass several stumps of ghost trees of the same scale, five or six feet in diameter.

A hundred years ago I would have seen a forest of many such trees—a more continuous forest, a wilder and more mysterious forest, more frightening maybe, more beautiful certainly. That diminishment is a loss. The widespread unloveliness of the scalped hills is a loss. No one flying over Oregon or the greater Northwest can miss the signature of the twentieth century, the crude geometry of clear-cuts and squiggly logging roads up and down the Coast Range, up and down the Cascades, splotched and spotted through the interior mountains clear to Hells Canyon. And the losses are not merely aesthetic. On too many slopes the stripped and road-cut soil has slid, ravaging habitat, silting streams. Native salmon and steelhead are struggling in the watersheds they've known as home for two million years.

But like any true story, the story of the land is complicated. I know a little more of it now that I've lived in rural Oregon for a while. The clear-cuts that tell of loss tell also of human livings made, food placed on tables, children raised. They tell of thousands of men such as those I once worked with, men who perform difficult and dangerous labor with spirit and skill. They tell of families maintaining themselves in communities and landscapes they love through three or four generations by means of work in the woods and mills. They tell of local economies that once thrived, though not many are thriving now. They tell of the philanthropic gifts of local mill owners. And—a part of the story that should be of keen interest to all of us—the clear-cuts tell of the work's product, the materials that have housed and comforted a nation.

In summer months I like to sip bourbon in the evening on our back deck, looking south into our neighbor Allen's trees, a stand of stately Douglas firs beginning to develop the mossy, open-park look of the old-growth condition. Sundown turns the green of boughs and moss intensely radiant, a green-gold stillness laced with the songs of finch and robin and Swainson's thrush. I enjoy this presence, never failing to feel lucky, on a deck my wife's son Chris constructed of Douglas fir posts and two-by-six lumber. The deck is attached to a house made of beams and studs and joists and rafters, of plywood sheathing and particleboard subfloor, of wood siding and molding and fascia boards. Inside the house we have wooden furniture, and we have books and magazines and writing pads and other kinds of paper derived from wood. Within our standing green grove and our neighbor's grove, which spare us the view of ugly clear-cuts, we live in a comfortable shell of clear-cut forest.

I'm glad for the trees I look at and glad for the trees that compose my house. And I'm uneasy, too, until the birds and the bourbon agreeably move my thoughts on, because I know I still don't get the story. I'm still trying to accept that I'm *in* the story, just as I'm in my creek bottom's story—that my choices or failures to choose and my acceptance of choices made by others are directly related to what I see and don't see from my deck, to what I can't help but see when I fly over my home state and region. On my deck or in the air, I sit where all of us sit, caught up comfortably or not in the dynamic and intricate balance between human use and natural beauty, between preservation of self and preservation of the wild, between the claims of economy and the claims of ecology, between the culture of rural localities and the culture of cities and suburbs. I sit squarely involved in a shifting field of human need and convenience and awareness and blindness that has drastically reshaped the face of the Northwest since Lewis and Clark paddled down the Columbia and continues to reshape it now, every day, for ourselves and for residents to come.

In 1992 I gave a reading at an annual conservationist get-together in the heart of eastern Oregon's ranch and timber country. One focus of the conference over the years had been the promotion of legislation that would create new designated wilderness areas and restrict cattle grazing on public lands east of the Cascades, legislation I supported then and support now. We walked out of the first morning session into a large and well-organized protest. Cattle trucks and log trucks had pulled up, festooned with banners, and more than a hundred men, women, and children stood along our pathway in disciplined silence, holding signs that labeled us as irresponsible outsiders who wanted the backcountry set aside as our playground and cared nothing for those who lived closer to the land and tried to make their livings from it.

I've been walking picket lines since I was a boy, some of them with my father on behalf of strikers. Now I was not a protester but an object of protest, and it stung. As my wife and I walked the silent gantlet, I muttered under my breath, stifling jibes and wisecracks. At one point my eyes met those of a stocky old man in overalls. He stared at me, unblinking, then slowly leaned forward and spat tobacco juice on the ground between us. I tried to reply in kind, but I had quit chewing when I'd quit logging. My mouth was dry, and my statement came out considerably less eloquent than his. Marilyn tugged me and we disappeared for lunch.

That was my first direct exposure to a kind of dem-
onstration that became commonplace in the 1990s
throughout the Northwest. Other acts of protest, less
disciplined and more violent, also have occurred. Dead
spotted owls have been left on the doorsteps of Forest
Service ranger stations. Someone, as yet unprosecuted,
torched nine thousand acres of forest in the central
Oregon Cascades to make the land available for salvage
logging. Environmental activists and federal employees
have been threatened and harassed. Some on the conservationist side have limited their actions to nonviolent
tree sittings and logging-road blockades, but others have
spiked trees and sabotaged heavy equipment. A Forest
Service pickup was burned. An arson fire that destroyed
an Oregon ranger station may have been set by a radical
underground network known as the Earth Liberation
Front. This group has claimed responsibility for many
recent acts of property destruction in the Northwest
and elsewhere.

As this hostile climate has developed, I've thought
about that 1992 protest and the spitting spat I had with
the old man. At the time and for months afterward, I
thought the protesters were wrong. Now I think they
were wrong in some ways and right in others. They were
wrong to believe that we who attended the conference,
and others of the green persuasions, are motivated solely
by elitist self-interest. We are concerned about the health
of the public lands, which constitute half the area of the
state of Oregon and a major portion of the West. In
many places those lands are in poor condition, mainly
because of excessive logging, grazing, and mining. Even
if they doubt our motives, the rural protesters would

bolster their credibility if they acknowledged what the land clearly attests—that over the course of the twentieth century, resource extraction has been too heavily favored over other land uses and values, including the land's ecological integrity. They need to accept, too, that the public lands are indeed public. We all share a legitimate interest in their management. And the protesters would do well to recognize that a necessary economic transition is occurring throughout the West, away from intensive extraction and toward a more diversified and sustainable economy, and that pressure from environmentalists is only one of the forces driving that change.

But "economic transition" is a phrase all too easy to mouth for those of us whose livelihoods aren't threatened by it and whose recreational interests are served by it. For many rural communities, the transition has felt like three body blows over the last quarter century. In the 1970s and 80s, automation began to take a toll in well-paying mill jobs. An increasingly globalized economy then destabilized the prices of forest and agricultural commodities. And, from the late 1980s on, federal agencies responded to conservationist lobbying and lawsuits by placing unprecedented limits on public-lands logging, which caused mill closures, more job losses, and the loss of millions of dollars in federal timber receipts returned to rural counties to support schools, roads, and other public purposes. All these changes have yielded failing businesses, depopulated communities, and the stress symptoms—increased depression, alcoholism, domestic violence—that inevitably occur when traditionally self-reliant people lose their economic independence.

Residents of the rural Northwest have suffered more and are angrier than many in the population centers are aware.

No class of workers can expect to be exempted from the vagaries of a market economy, but ranch and timber workers might find the transition more palatable if we conservationists more forthrightly acknowledged our own implication in and insulation from natural resource economics. We decry injuries to the environment, but we participate in those injuries by consuming the goods that come of them, and we expect those goods to remain available at affordable prices. Many of us blanch at any rough handling of nature, not knowledgeable enough to distinguish appropriate use from irresponsible overuse or abuse. We may be well versed in ecology, but we are more or less ignorant of practical economy, the techniques by which the necessaries of human life are derived from the natural world. Not many suburbanites with environmentalist sympathies know how to fall a tree and turn it into usable lumber, how to pull a calf or raise a crop of grain or fill the hold of a boat with salmon. The tasks and responsibilities of practical economy have become abstract for us, though our dependence on their products is quite concrete.

Nor do we know, most of us, what it means to live for three or four generations in the same community and countryside. Many rural Northwesterners do. They inhabit the same portion of landscape, sometimes the same town or ranch or plot of land, where their parents and grandparents lived and worked and hunted and fished and raised their kids. It should be understandable enough that the present dwellers want to raise their own kids there; without work, however, many are finding it necessary to relocate and retrain for new jobs—usually poorer paying than the jobs they lost—in the tourism and high-tech industries. To leave home means something considerably more profound to a third-generation millhand from Burns or Oakridge than to a software consultant, say, who is used to and perhaps even welcomes the life of gliding from job to job in various cities. In timber country, t-shirts that say LOGGERS ARE AN ENDANGERED SPECIES are common. They are not a joke to those who wear them. We who speak and act in the name of the wild communities need to appreciate that authentic human communities too are crumbling under the pressure of progress.

The story of the twentieth century in rural America has been the emptying of its populations into the cities. In agriculture, as Wendell Berry has been pointing out for decades, this has meant nothing good for small farmers *or* for the health of the land. The same is likely to prove true in ranch and timber country. The decisions that have injured the forests and rangelands of the Northwest were made for the most part by corporations and the federal government, not by workers and owners of small holdings. I remember old-timers grumbling thirty years ago that Weyerhaeuser was stripping its timber holdings too fast and wasn't replanting as it should. Many timber workers today will acknowledge that portions of the national forests have been overlogged. They drive the back roads to hunt and fish. They see the stripped mountainsides, some of them nearly as steep as cliffs, streaked with gullies and puke-outs. They see the muddy streams. They know that salmon and steelhead runs, with sporadic annual exceptions, have dwindled drastically.

But those workers did not force federal and state land-management agencies to sell far too much timber in the last fifty years, nor did they prompt Congress to fund annual harvests even higher than those agencies requested. Now that harvest levels have been sharply reduced, the national forests have begun, perhaps, a slow recovery. They will have a better chance, it seems to me, if the small communities in and around them survive—communities of long-term residents who care about where they live, who are part of the countryside and want to remain so. They are doing the best they can to diversify their economies, but as long as Americans use wood it will be necessary to cut trees, and it's perfectly appropriate that some of those trees should come from previously logged public forest lands that can sustain further logging, at least until replanted private timber can make up the difference. As for the many public sites that never should have been logged in the first place, they need restoration. If the government ever gets as serious about restoring forests as it was about leveling them, it will find workers with the necessary skills available.

Demonstrators—the dignified and the crude, the peaceful and the violent—are usually people who feel they are not being heard. Conservationists know exquisitely well what it feels like not to be heard. Our messages are getting out a bit better these days, and the evolving demographics of the West are bringing us greater influence, greater political power. As that occurs, we're obliged to keep our own ears perked for voices of dissent. I personally favor more designated wilderness in my state. I would like to see the last roadless areas in our public forests remain roadless. I would like to see reduced grazing near streams and in other sensitive areas. I would like to see meaningful mining reform. But there are members of the land community who disagree, and they, like me, are entitled to be heard, taken seriously, and understood. Spitting at each other won't get us far.

A few years ago, I was driving through country not far from the ranch where I used to live. It was early March, and the forested peaks—Gearhart, Saddle Mountain, Yainax Butte—still bore the lonely, snowy blue aspect of winter. The lower country, sage and juniper flats patched with pines, was mostly free of snow but still sleeping in its grays, browns, and drab greens. I stopped to walk by the Sycan River, which rises in the meadowy woods north of Gearhart, flows north and west to the Sycan Marsh, and winds south from there through pines and pasture to join the Sprague River near the town of Beatty.

The signatures of the landscape were pleasurably familiar. The river's roiling tannic current with its laughing riffles. Clumps of native bunchgrass among lichened boulders. Lodgepole pines in small stands, the wet duff of their needles fragrant and yielding underfoot, their spent cones crunching. A few tall ponderosas, most wildly beautiful of trees, trunks vibrantly orange. And high in their crowns, singing through numberless boughs of long green needles, the wind's old anthem of solitude and space.

To my eyes and heart, that country is the prettiest in Oregon. In fact, it's the prettiest country I know. I was in no hurry to leave it, so a little later I pulled the truck over at a roadside tavern, a small annex to a general store a few miles east of Chiloquin. The place had a four-stool bar and half a dozen tables. A woman and three men, all in their fifties or sixties, were talking at one of the tables. The woman padded behind the bar in her slippers and served me the beer I ordered.

She and the men resumed their conversation, talking along in the easy manner of friends. Someone had sighted a bear. Someone's shed had burned. One of the men was going to keep his tomatoes in a cold frame all summer. "*Let* it frost," he said. This set off a round of wry comments about the weather they shared and endured. "I don't believe we'll get more snow," said one. "Oh, *now* you've done it," shot back another, and they all laughed. It was satisfying to hear their pained affection. I remembered Wallace Stegner grumping about his clay soil: "Too hard in summer, too heavy in winter. There's a week in the fall and a week in the spring you can work this stuff." And Wendell Berry, shaking his head after Cane Run had flooded a cornfield three springs in a row: "I believe I'll quit making suggestions to that field."

The woman was talking now, about a friend who had recently moved up from Los Angeles. "You know what she says about it here, what she loves?" the woman asked, pausing to draw on her cigarette and relish the pleasure of what she was about to report. "She says, 'Up here, I've got room to *fluff!*'"

I laughed with the four of them, savoring the friend's remark and the woman's delight in telling it. All of us who live in the Northwest, I thought to myself, must feel some version of the same pleasure. Whether it's physical space we most value, or the informal sociability, or the less frenetic pace of life, or the freedom to be different, or all of those, we have room here, room to shake and plump our feathers and feel all right. It involves much more than landscape, but the possibility of such fluffing room begins in landscape—in an uncrowded countryside enjoyed by those who live and make their livings there, and enjoyed recreationally by those who choose to live, or have little choice but to live, in our cities and suburbs. And it begins even more fundamentally in the preservation of wilder landscapes, places where all human beings are visitors, not residents.

I broke out of such thoughts when the woman padded behind the bar again and served me a glass of beer I hadn't ordered. One of the men had taken a seat at the other end of the bar. He smiled and touched the bill of his cap, which bore the logo of a heavy machinery company. "Passing through?" he asked.

"Passing through," I answered. "I used to live down near Bonanza."

"Poe Valley?"

"Langell Valley."

"Were you ranching?"

"My friends were ranching. I was admiring the scenery."

He grinned. "That's nice work. I get down to hunt near Bly some years. Pretty country."

"Pretty country here, too," I said.

"Oh my," the man said. "Doesn't get any better."

We talked on for a while, exchanging pleasantries, the man politely trying to discover what had brought me to the bar and to the country where he lived. I didn't tell him, because I feared it would chill the friendliness of our encounter. I had stopped to renew my acquaintance with the Sycan River because I was writing the text for a photograph book about Oregon rivers protected by state and federal law. Among other angles, I was writing about the human abuses of rivers that have made government protections necessary and may necessitate more.

Our talk tailed off. I thanked the man for the beer he had bought me and left the genial company of the tavern, regretting my cowardice. Because I feared what he might think of me—and, I suppose, what I might think of him—if our views and purposes had become known, I had declined to tell a friendly inquirer what I was doing in his part of the state. I should have told him. We should have talked about rivers and followed wherever the rivers took us. We might have disagreed about the condition of Oregon's streams and forests and rangeland and about who should manage them and how, but we had something more important in common. We knew the same landscape, and we loved it. Love may seem an impossibly vague trail to common ground, but what other do we have? If the man in the cap and I and all earnest people who care about the future of the land could recognize and honor the love for the land we all share despite our differences, maybe we could talk things through without spitting or shouting. Maybe we'd find there's work we can do together. Maybe we'd find there's work we can only do together.

THE UNTELLABLE STORY

I don't remember when or how the concept of evolution first entered my awareness, but it probably came as history rather than biology. My father, who had been a socialist in the 1930s, still liked to think in terms of the Marxian dialectic as I was growing up, so it's likely I absorbed at an early age a sense that historical progress is a function of struggles between opposite forces. I seem to remember my father telling me about the Scopes trial—Clarence Darrow was one of his heroes—but the issue as argued at the trial was pretty crude, and my grasp of it even cruder. It seemed there were two possibilities. Humans had been created by the God of the Bible, or humans had descended from apes. (Who had created the apes, or what they had descended from, I don't recall hearing.) Some of my boyhood friends belittled the descent-from-apes theory, and I very likely belittled it too. It wasn't comfortable or even very plausible to young boys with noticeable hair only on their heads, though I do remember the thought of it crossing my mind once in the dressing room of the community swimming pool as I watched a thoroughly hairy man take off his clothes and pull on his trunks.

My friends and I were familiar with the phrase "survival of the fittest," and it was by that phrase that we understood, or misunderstood, evolution. My interest in Jack London's novels must have strengthened the notion that only the strongest survive, and only through bloody struggle. This did not bode well for a quiet kid who liked books and hated to fight, so I didn't think about it much. Just because it might be true for dogs and wolves, I reasoned, and maybe for poor workers and rich bosses, didn't mean it was true for me.

It's hard to believe that the topic of evolution never came up in eighth-grade science or ninth-grade biology, but if it did I don't recall it. Maybe the subject was still too charged for teachers and textbooks in the early 1960s. Though I was aware that people disagreed strongly on the question of human origins, I had no strong feelings of my own. I was raised with some exposure to the theology and imaginal flavor of Christianity, but no practice of it other than a few sessions of Unitarian Sunday school and an occasional midnight service at one church or another on Christmas Eve. The first few lines of Genesis, the Twenty-third Psalm, and portions of the Gospels were the only parts of the Bible I would have recognized. I had a brief love affair with the Christ story when I was fourteen, but my emotional intensity quickly backslid into fishing, baseball, and eventually girls. In the absence of a religious faith or a scientific understanding of evolution, I didn't dwell on human origins. When I looked beyond the busy and problematic present I looked always forward, toward the uncertain but tantalizing future, and toward my personal future, the only one that really counted.

It was Loren Eiseley, in *The Immense Journey,* who first showed me the vastness of time and made me feel part of the evolutionary work of time. His book, which I came to while in high school, moved me not because he explained evolution—he didn't—but because he imagined it. He put the theory into images and the images into a story, an epic narrative in which humankind was only one character. It didn't bother me a bit to learn that we may have descended from a small, rodentlike mammal that burrowed in the ground, a "shabby little Paleocene rat, eternal tramp and world wanderer, father of all mankind." I *liked* having that guy in my lineage—it was like having an unsavory and quite colorful great uncle in the family. Because of him I felt a little closer to the woodchucks and squirrels I saw on my Blue Ridge rambles and even learned a little respect for Uncle Tom, the rat who was a permanent tenant and true proprietor of our cabin. And I liked it that this great uncle's own great uncles had evaded by night the towering Reptiles—or evaded them frequently enough, in any case—and that even earlier ancestors had spent fifty million years or so in "the green twilight of the rain forest," acquiring hands that gripped and eyes that focused as one and saw the world in color. The story of evolution shed light on many things, including my childhood love of climbing trees.

That Eiseley was a paleontologist strengthened his authority, but it was the saga, not the science, that excited me. He provided me—and, I'm sure, many others without religious belief—with a creation narrative. Or better, an emergence narrative. Eiseley, like Darwin before him, didn't claim to know or to be able to know the origin of life. In this way their evolution story resembles those Native American tales that presuppose the existence of a raw world and tell how humans emerged out of and into that world—ascending through a series of underground rooms in the Zuni story, issuing from a hollow log in the Kiowa version. Evolution also imagines life emerging from the planet's womb—coalescing somehow as simple forms in the ocean deeps, proliferating throughout the seas, making landfall eventually and colonizing the continents, and producing in time as part of its prodigious array at least one species able to look back and wonder at the story and try to piece it together from the incomplete evidence available.

Eiseley led my imagination not just to the evolution of life but to the older and vaster stories of geology and cosmology. The big bang theory was getting a lot of attention as I grew up, suggesting strongly that not only life on Earth but the physical universe itself was an evolutionary phenomenon, originating from a single source and developing over the course of thousands of millions of years. Somehow, it began to occur to me, every story must live within other stories, from grains of sand on the Carolina coast to the sun and moon to the farthest stars and beyond, and all must be encompassed in one infinite story. Though I couldn't grasp or define that story, or even the smaller ones that composed it, I knew I believed in it, and though I still can't grasp or define it, I believe in it now. Science and religion and poetry show flashes of it. In Nature I sense the story everywhere, and beauty is the best name I know for it. I don't mean grace or symmetry or sublimity or any other particular measure of beauty, but all of those and more—the beauty of wholeness, of stars and land and the forms of life precisely as Nature has made them and is making them now, the beauty that Emily Dickinson called "nature's fact." This is the oldest beauty, the beauty essential to the meaning of the Greek term *kosmos*, the beauty whose derivation as a word relates it to "bounty" and ultimately to the Sanskrit *duvas*, meaning "reverence" or "gift." The beauty of the given world. The beauty that is always a becoming, life and death both dancing to it, one long and varied gesture reaching through time.

Evolution has become my faith, and I mean that word in its full religious significance. To have faith is to trust with confidence in the unseen. I trust the unseen movement of being by which the universe gave birth to our sun and planet, by which they gave birth to life, and by which life has elaborated into a diverse wholeness we are only beginning to know. There is strong evidence supporting evolution as scientific theory, but believing in evolution as I imagine it is still a matter of faith. I have never seen one species of life transform into another. I can't prove that the homologous forelimbs of amphibians and birds and bats and whales and humans all derive from a common ancestor, or that the development of the human embryo recapitulates the evolutionary metamorphosis of fish into amphibian into reptile into mammal. I can't prove that I like to climb trees and am physiologically equipped for it because epochs ago my great-great-uncles lived off the ground in African forests.

And, needless to say, neither I nor anyone else has performed the neat trick of turning a beaker of amino acids into a living creature. Charles Darwin acknowledged and evidently was untroubled by his own unscientific faith concerning ultimate origins. "There is grandeur in this view of life," he wrote in *The Origin of Species,* "having been originally breathed by the Creator into a few forms or into one," from which "endless forms most beautiful and most wonderful have been, and are being evolved." Loren Eiseley cited no Creator as author of the evolutionary journey, but confessed his own faith in a "mysterious principle known as 'organization'": "Like some dark and passing shadow within matter, it cups out the eyes' small windows or spaces the notes of a meadowlark's song in the interior of a mottled egg. That principle—I am beginning to suspect—was there before the living in the deeps of water."

Any account of the origin of life or the origin of being, whether religious or scientific or a blend of both, is necessarily an imagining of faith. The biblical story of Genesis is one such imagining, a beautiful one that shapes my life and work, I am sure, in more ways than I know. I admire its orderly progression, the sure and stately way it depicts an evolution of its own. God calls forth light from darkness, heaven and dry land from the formless waters, grasses and herbs and fruit trees from the land, swimming and flying creatures from the oceans, and cattle and other terrestrial animals after their kinds from the fresh and green-growing earth. All of this is good in the eyes of God, but only humans are specifically said to have been made in God's image. I've always stumbled on that part of the story. In my late twenties, five unexceptional words in the writings of C. G. Jung rang my spirit like a bell: "God wants to become man," he wrote, referring to the Christ story. Not man, I thought, but God wants to *become*. God materializes, incarnates himself in matter, to realize the fullness of his being in the evolving panoply of the cosmos. He did not design the universe but desires it, the way a poet desires the poem he can't yet see and finds its design only in its making. God finds his way only as we and the rest of creation find ours. And so, being extends itself in ever developing orders of wholeness that form and dissolve in death and then re-form, inhabiting possibility with the amplitude of all that is.

Or so I imagine it, but there are only two things I hold certain. Being is a miracle, and the true nature of the miracle is beyond our knowing. The terms and categories we employ when talking about ultimate things, including "beauty," "wholeness," "God," "evolution," and others I use, are crude signifiers, markers made of clay. To speak of mind or matter or design or desire or chance or necessity is to peer through a lens that distorts other regions of the truth as it brings a particular region into focus. In the nineteenth century no one doubted the distinction between matter and energy; now, to physicists at least, that difference has melted. I suspect that other distinctions we habitually assume, including that between the animate and the inanimate, will turn out to tell more about the limits of rational analytic thinking than they tell about the nature of being.

And that's just as well. Like poetry and all art, stories live by suggestion, not explanation, and in that way the greatest story, the story of being, lives in our minds and hearts. To be alive is to hear and tell stories, and the stories are as alive as we are. They change in the hearing and telling. They change as we live on in our lives, as humankind lives farther into time. They will not be restrained in static versions. Maybe the only truly impoverished souls are the rigidly orthodox, whether religious or scientific—those so obsessed with the text of a single story that they deny the validity of others and lose sight of the beauty their own story is meant to suggest, not to contain. The great feast ready before them, they gnaw instead on the meager nourishment of the menu.

"Talk of mysteries!" wrote Thoreau, all stirred up on a Maine mountain. "Think of our life in nature,—daily to be shown matter, to come in contact with it,—rocks, trees, wind on our cheeks! the *solid* earth! the *actual* world!" If you follow the physicists, the actual world is made of willful little particles with names like "quark" and "gluon" that dodge into and out of existence, enlivening a universe born some fifteen billion years ago from a single seed of space and time, an evolving universe that has composed itself into nebulas, stars, planets, and Thoreau with wind on his cheeks. If you follow the Bible or another good book you may imagine the story differently, but whatever the story you see by, the world is here, impossible and undeniable, its own most eloquent explanation. We belong to a mystery that does not belong to us, yet it is freely granted, everywhere and all the time. We distance ourselves, we fail to see, but the mystery does not fail us. It spirals through the molecules of our own DNA, through the shells of snails and the chambered nautilus, through the grain of junipers and the great spinning storms and the spiral arms of the Milky Way, and so joins itself to the infinite from which it arose.

Though life on Earth has tended over the course of its four billion years toward greater organic complexity, it was not inevitable that any particular species of complex organism should have come into being, including our own. We were happened upon, not planned. But we were carefully crafted, too. The raw materials of evolution, genetic mutations, arise by chance, but each is preserved or discarded by natural selection according to its survival value for the species—an unintentional but exhaustive design process of innumerable incremental changes over the eons. Looking back in time through the fossil record, we can read certain passages of a narrative leading to our human existence. We can see, for instance, that the occurrence among certain fish of four lobelike fins on the lower body, useful for stabilization in currents and for mobility in shallow pools, enabled those fish in times of drought to clamber from one shrinking water hole to another, sucking harsh air into primitive lungs, and led through further adaptive mutations to amphibians with paired fore fins and hind fins, to walking reptiles and quadruped mammals, and eventually to our two-legged kind.

A human life too is unpredictable at its outset, and is shaped by accidents of experience and unconscious forces as much as by an individual's conscious will, but looking back from any point along the way, a pattern, an evolution, is detectable. As Loren Eiseley opened my imagination to the evolution of life at large, the writings of Jung on individuation helped me see that a single life also is an organic movement tending toward wholeness of being. I think of my own life as a tree that will grow as full as its nature and circumstances allow, touching air and soil with every leaf and rootlet it can produce. Like the one lanky oak of my home acre, the tree of my being is ungainly, its trunk crooked, its crown uneven. It is missing limbs that might have grown but didn't, others that started to grow but stopped, still others that grew and were broken in the weather of experience. But its trunk and limbs and leaves and unseen roots, such as they are, do compose a unique embodiment of wholeness, a wholeness toward which the tree in its advancing age still tends. The simpler, suppler wholeness of youth is gone, but the more accomplished wholeness of age, for all its eccentricity and scarrings and brittleness, may be better able to take in and appreciate the mystery of being. It is the paradox of age that the closer I come to my death, the better suited I feel for living.

And if my life is an evolution, so too is this essay. I didn't plan or foresee it as I've written it, but discovered it page by page, moving from memory to memory, thought to thought, as one has suggested another, looking for the pattern of a personal natural history. No artistic attempt, even in the genre we call nonfiction, can be born fully whole. It must evolve. It must come into being as an animal grows into mature shapeliness, as children at play invent a new game, as coalescing nebular dust takes fire as an infant star. The conscious mind intentionally shapes the material as the pattern comes clearer, but the material itself and its essential form must come from beyond the small lit room of awareness—from the wilderness of the greater psyche, which opens, in some way, into the wild universe itself. It is the artist's gift and privilege to bear into wholeness, in A. R. Ammons's phrase, "the forms / things want to come as," and in so doing the artist echoes and affirms the evolutionary energy of life and the cosmos itself. That is the joy at the heart of writing or of any art, even art that tells of personal anguish or monstrous evil. In bringing work to wholeness its maker drinks from the original fountain, the mystery that gave birth to all that is. That, I believe, is what Ralph Waldo Emerson had in mind when he defined a poem as "a thought so passionate and alive that like the spirit of a plant or an animal it has an architecture of its own, and adorns Nature with a new thing."

That aim, of course, scrapes continually against the limits of one's talent and character and against the limits of the medium one works in. And for nature writers—for this one, at least—it can yield a paradoxical effect. Many people love the lives and things of Nature and draw deep satisfaction from them without needing to render their experience into art or even into language. The experience itself is sufficient. But for me the experience, however vivid or gratifying or moving, often isn't sufficient. I need to tell about it, to rub it in memory for latent color and luster, to praise or lament or wonder— to transmute the experience into verbal art. Or maybe the need is even more basic. Maybe I need language to fully realize the experience itself, as if I haven't truly heard the thrush sing until it sings in my poem, a poem that comes from the woods by way of the pencil in my right hand. I need to sing back in order to hear the original song. And then, when I hear a thrush again, I hear it through the sounding board of my poem. The making that draws me closer to Nature also divides me from it.

The problem may not be that language falsifies experience, as I worried in my twenties, but that to one extent or another language can come to replace experience. This is the predicament of all writers who seek to communicate in a representational way what has happened to them in their lives, and it may be nothing more than the broader predicament of the human mind itself. Consciousness, though it seems to place us continuously in the moving present, is actually playing hurried catch-up the whole time, a moving picture of what just *was* the present. Except in deep meditational states, consciousness is already memory, and those contents of consciousness that persist in memory are themselves constantly and unconsciously revised, a fabrication continually refabricated, from which the writer necessarily fabricates further as he shapes remembered experience into art.

All of which leaves me, as I sit at this desk in my study and scrawl with my pencil, pretty far removed from the Douglas fir boughs stirring soundlessly in a light breeze outside the window. I love the living world, but I've probably truly known it only in moments. I knew it as the rattlesnakes buzzed beneath me, and later that day as I looked west from the Blue Ridge. I knew it as an incandescent tree at the top of Sentinel Rock. I knew it near the end of a fourteen-hour ski trip around Crater Lake, when, my defenses worn down by thirty miles of fatigue, the grandeur of alpenglow on the snowy slopes brought tears. I knew it as I crawled three miles to my truck after breaking my ankle at Castle Crags. I've known it a few times under the influence of psychedelic drugs, in that all too fleeting interval when the rigidity of personal identity has dissolved and fear has yet to set in. I've known it in moments of sexual intensity. And I've known it in ordinary moments, mostly in childhood, when I've felt spontaneously withdrawn from time into a presence I can only call eternity.

Creative writing feels to me like a way of groping in language toward the unshuttered clarity of those moments. Not toward the re-creation of a particular one necessarily, but toward the moment's transparent intensity, its quality of revelatory seeing, its *knowing*. It can't be captured in words, but words can suggest it, point to it, reveal its presence the way aspen leaves shimmer with a breeze the skin can't sense, the way an almost imperceptible dimpling on the surface of a puddle shows the falling of unfelt rain. In that way, I hope, the things I write lead me back to the primary world they divide me from. Much in our world of human artifice is not real. Much that our world has caused us to forget is very real. I write to touch and to be touched by the real, and I try to write in such a way that a reader or listener who doesn't know me can enter the things I make and find his or her own sense of the real enlivened. Writing in this sense is a gift. It is one way of contributing to the human community in time, to this ongoing conversation we are having about who we are, where we are and where we have come from, who and what our neighbors are, and how our lives should matter.

It's September as I write this, and as in past Septembers, Marilyn and I are picking blackberries in the creek bottom that forms the lower half of our acre. We have three varieties: the native creeping blackberry, sometimes called dewberry; the exotic but fairly docile evergreen version; and the exotic and highly aggressive Himalayan variety, the kind that spreads its exuberant thorny canes along the margins of fields and roadways and backyards all across the wet regions of the Northwest. If all of us left and returned ten years later, we'd find only the taller trees and the rooftops of some of our houses protruding from one continuous brambly wilderness of Himalayan blackberry.

It's a misleading name. The species may or may not

have roots in the Himalaya, but it definitely came to North America from England, where it was bred and developed by Luther Burbank in the late nineteenth century. Its presence here parallels the presence of people like me, humans of European ancestry who have overrun the landscape even more thoroughly and flamboyantly than the blackberry hordes. I used to think poorly of both invaders, the zoological and the botanical. Both have run rampant, both have done damage to native populations. But there's no rewinding the spool of history, and no quantity of guilt, regret, or blackberry poison is going to revise the story to date. Both invaders are here to stay, and neither is all bad. Most Euro-Americans in the Northwest are earnest people trying to live responsible lives, whatever their forebears may have done, here or elsewhere. And as for the Anglo-Himalayan berries, they lack the intense spicy flavor of the smaller native variety, but this September, as in Septembers past, they taste pretty damn good.

In 1994, when we moved here, the creek bottom was choked with blackberry thickets. Our neighbor Allen, who has a small organic farm, offered to help clear them with his tractor. He mowed the thickets and then raked the ground to turn up the roots, which we collected and burned. That was a start. "The roots you've missed will let you know," Allen told us, and they did, sending up shoots within weeks. We've kept after them, erratically, and now, six years later, we're close to an acceptable armistice. We've beaten the putative Himalayans back to the fence line between our place and Allen's, where they make a rough but nice enough hedgerow, and to an enclave on the north side of the acre where the creek flows in, and another on the south where it flows out. Most of the bottom is now open to our own suggestions, not just Luther Burbank's, and we still get all the berries we can eat and freeze at the end of every summer.

It was midsummer when Allen helped us, and the creek was dry. I remember wishing out loud that it ran year-round. "It does," said Allen, gesturing at the riot of biomass he had mowed. "The winter creek flows all year. Plant your tomatoes here and they won't need water."

I think of his comment every June when the creek channel lapses into mud and the blackberries open their white blossoms, the thickets humming with attentive bees. Through July and August, as the channel dries completely, hard green berries swell and darken on the leafy canes. In late August we pop the first ripe ones into our mouths, each berry plump and purple, each softly swollen cell giving up sweet juice to the gentlest pressure of our tongues. The berries are drops from the secret stream; my tomatoes and cucumbers are larger poolings. We drink from the dark life that flows beneath us, that follows its given way all summer and half the fall among particles of soil and stone, among roots and the tunnelings of creatures that never see light, as we walk and mow and plant and weed and harvest in the bright dry world above. I can't see the stream and can't hear it, but in my imagination it flows from far away—clear from northern Virginia, from the murmuring underground river, its voice verging on speech, that passed through my hearing and dreams forty years ago when I was a boy.

If I hunger less now than I did then, it's not because I know more, but because everywhere now I find evidence of the unseen. Like the purloined letter, it hides in its own conspicuousness. My own stained fingers prove its presence, and so does my blood when I reach too quickly for a cluster of berries and rake my wrist on a thorny cane. Every creekside weed and wildflower betokens the unseen. Every fern and forb and spike of grass, every stone in the dry creek bed bespeaks its being, which I cannot name and do not need to name. I may know more about a wildflower after looking it up in a book, but I won't know the flower itself better. I may know it less—I may stop seeing it in its own peculiar light when I hold it by a name inside my head. It's the bloom itself I want, *this* bloom, its particular crooked stem and one of its pink petals askew, the surprise of it by the path to the shed in the slant light of late afternoon.

My mother, in her last years, had a way sometimes of gazing intensely, fiercely even, at familiar things— birds, fruits, persons—whose names her eroded cognitive mind could not recall. And yet in some way, I often thought, she saw them truly—saw further into their undefinable mystery than I did, with their names nimble on my tongue. "But nature is a stranger yet," wrote Emily Dickinson,

> The ones that cite her most
> Have never passed her haunted house,
> Nor simplified her ghost.
>
> To pity those that know her not
> Is helped by the regret
> That those who know her, know her less
> The nearer her they get.

I get nearer and nearer, and I know Nature less and less by what I write and what I read. Something in me, something wiser than I am, may be preparing me for the time when I will wholly rejoin her. No names will be useful to me then. No poem or essay or story I've written or could write, those acts of naming I've made the work of my life, will be helpful or even meaningful. I'll be done with menus then; I'll have become, quite literally, the meal. I will go down to the secret stream, whose expressions in the sunlit world I once walked among and praised and sometimes cursed, once took into my body and toasted with a purple tongue. I will enter the unseen, and I will see, perhaps, that I never left it, or perhaps will see nothing at all, or will see in ways I can't now imagine.

I'm in no hurry. I've come a good long way to my place, and, whatever its measurement in time, I have a good way ahead. I wander less now than I did in my youth, but I am very much in motion. I have learned that there is no end to love, that love calls always to further love, and I am learning that there is no end to finding home. I am here and still arriving here, still alert for hints and clues, still listening for Winter Creek's first November lilt and for the speechfulness of its summer quiet. For me it's been important and remains important to devote my attention to this true dream in which I've awakened, to take an outward way through a little of the world's wildness toward the wholeness of self and place. I am not likely to know what the world is trying to be. It is enough, it is plenty, to be one small parcel of Nature's becoming, to see just that glimpse of the story I am capable of seeing and to write what I am capable of writing. It is enough, it is plenty and more than plenty, standing at night beneath nameless stars as a slow wind stirs the treetops, to know that the power that imagined me and all things into being stirs through us and beyond, far past our own imaginings of what it is, and beautiful is the flowing of its song.

JOHN DANIEL

A PORTRAIT

by Scott Slovic

> *Anything in nature reflects the viewer, but of all the
> natural forms, rivers give back the fullest reflection of
> the human. They are lives in motion, bound up like
> ours in time and consequence, steadily being born and
> steadily dying. They stir in their sleep, they laugh and
> mourn, and—like us at our best—they are true to them-
> selves under all conditions, changeful and changeless,
> free and constrained, a resurgent presence of past and
> future made one.*

—John Daniel, "The Spirit of Rivers"

Nestled between Spencer Butte at its southern end and
Skinner Butte just north of downtown, perched along
the winding Willamette River, which empties Cascade
snowmelt to the Pacific Ocean, Eugene, Oregon, is a
quintessential western college town. The University of
Oregon draws eighteen thousand students each year,
and coffee shops and used bookstores cluster near campus to cater to the students and faculty and others who
savor the informal, outdoorsy, intellectual ambience.
Forty years ago, there were about twenty thousand
people in all of Eugene; today, the Eugene-Springfield

area is a bustling minimetropolis of some two hundred thousand. The city struggles to balance its evergreen hillsides with the demands of growth and development.

Fifteen miles west of Eugene in the direction of the coast is a man-made lake called Fern Ridge Reservoir, and just west of the reservoir are the hamlets of Veneta and Elmira. Scattered wooden houses dot the pasturelands or retire from sight in remaining groves of Douglas firs. Convenience stores and other small businesses line the main road, but most people out here live lives of quiet seclusion. This is a realm of country roads, birdsong, the steady tap-tapping of rainfall much of the year, and the visual experience of infinite shades of the color green. Green grass, green ferns, green blackberry bushes, green moss on the trunks of evergreen trees. This is a good place to think, to wallow in soggy depression during the cloudy months, and to celebrate the profusion of life when sunlight breaks through now and then and for the summer months.

Here, in the foothills of Oregon's Coast Range, a few stone throws from the Long Tom River, John Daniel has made his home since 1994.

Lorraine Anderson begins her 1996 sketch of Daniel's life and work for the Scribner reference book *American Nature Writers* by noting the title essay of Daniel's 1992 collection, *The Trail Home,* in which he mentions that he has lived in twenty-nine different dwellings during his first forty years. Twenty-nine. The purpose of this revelation was not to celebrate itinerancy and unattachment, nor to single out himself as a uniquely rootless man. Instead, as is often the goal of his writing, Daniel tries in this lyrical meditation to explain an idea about his life that he has come, somewhat to his surprise, to notice. The effect is humbling rather than self-laudatory. In "The Trail Home," written in the late 1980s while Daniel was living in a guest cottage next to Wallace Stegner's home in Los Altos Hills, California, and working as a Jones Lecturer in creative writing at Stanford University, Daniel subtly argues against the call for a rooted sense of place that Stegner himself seemed to advocate. For example, Stegner's essay "The Sense of Place" opens with the following statement:

> If you don't know where you are, says Wendell Berry, you don't know *who* you are. Berry is a writer, one of our best, who after some circling has settled on the bank of the Kentucky River, where he grew up and where his family has lived for many generations. . . . He calls himself a "placed" person.

Stegner later specifies what he thinks Berry means by "knowing where you are":

> He is talking about the kind of knowing that involves the senses, the memory, the history of a family or a tribe. He is talking about the knowledge of place that comes from working in it in all weathers, making a living from it, suffering from its catastrophes, loving its mornings or evenings or hot noons, valuing it for the profound investment of labor and feeling that you, your parents and grandparents, your all-but-unknown ancestors have put into it. He is talking about the knowing that poets specialize in.

And he concludes by arguing that Americans must learn to "submit" themselves to the places they live and experience in order to realize "the sense of place" and establish "a sustainable relationship between people and earth." Stegner also mentions, in passing, "I doubt that we will ever get the motion out of the American, for everything in his culture of opportunity and abundance has, up to now, urged motion on him as a form of virtue." There is an unspoken frustration in this essay, an inability to resolve the desire for placed responsibility and the realization of American mobility. In a series of trenchant essays, John Daniel takes the baton from his friends and mentors, Stegner and Berry, and offers insightful and consoling meditations on mobility, stability, and the American experience of place.

Daniel opens "The Trail Home" by watching through binoculars as a neighbor in Los Altos Hills putters around the yard of his ostentatious new home. The purpose of the field glasses is to scan for wildlife, in particular a certain "red-shouldered hawk that yelps like a puppy." But as usual in John Daniel's work, the inspection comes closer to home, to the plights and predicaments of his own species, his family, and sometimes himself. He sees his neighbor walking around somewhat aimlessly, perplexed: "A man was puttering around the place, planting shrubs and flowers in raw slopes of dirt, piling construction scraps. For long intervals he would stand still, looking around, then he'd move to plant something else." In this most mundane of activities, his anonymous neighbor's tentative gardening gestures, Daniel senses one of the deepest human impulses: "It seemed to me he was trying to make connection with his new home, trying to locate himself as he located his plants. He was testing the ground with roots."

"Anything in nature reflects the viewer" is the opening phrase of Daniel's coda to the 1997 book, *Oregon Rivers*, a cluster of natural history essays joined with Larry N. Olson's lush photographs of the state's waterways. The passage goes on to suggest that of all nature's features, rivers offer the "fullest" reflection of what is human. Daniel's characteristic practice is to find in most aspects of the external world implications for the human realm and, in many dimensions of human experience, angles of unrest and illumination regarding his own life and identity. The observations at the beginning of "The Trail Home" are no exception. After observing his neighbor's planting movements, he pivots to reflect on his own activities: "The little framed vegetable plot I tend on our own hillside is the same kind of attempt. It's gaining the force of ritual with me, to put in a garden anyplace I expect to stay long enough to taste what I plant." The implication, early in this essay, is that long stays are not guaranteed and that even a residence long enough to taste a single harvest is worth savoring.

The next paragraph is, I would argue, one of the key statements in John Daniel's entire oeuvre—it sums up not only his methodology as a writer, but his vision of our mobile culture. I quote it to my students semester after semester:

> I don't know what the man of the pink villa was thinking this afternoon, but as I watched him standing there, looking around, drifting on to another job of planting or cleaning up, I imagined that he was trying to learn a language, the same language I want to learn. Or want to remember. Many around the world speak it clearly, precisely,

naturally—but the villa-man and I, and millions of others in this country where the average family moves once every four years, have a hard time with it. We skim freely from place to place, home to home, reasonably happy and very possessive of our independence, but also just a bit baffled, a bit stifled in our easy movement, sure of what belongs to us but not at all sure of what we belong to. Fluent in mobility, we try haltingly to learn the alphabet of place.

At the time when he wrote these words, Daniel was still living in a condition of long-term transience, renting a cottage on the property of Wallace and Mary Stegner. Dwelling number twenty-nine would inevitably give way to number thirty at some point in the future, and then number thirty-one. His attitude of desire, rather than self-satisfied achievement, is what gives particular poignancy to such phrases as "the same language I want to learn"—the "alphabet of place" has not yet been mastered by the author, just as most of us in this culture bumble and bungle our efforts to fit our environments comfortably, sustainably. Daniel is able, by watching the world carefully and then pulling observations back into the context of his own experience, his own yearning, to feel our pulse, too, and take its measure. His voice is at once self-deprecating and prophetically authoritative.

"The Trail Home" suggests that one way to learn the language of place is to "stop skimming and settle down." In contrast to himself, the author has friends who have managed to do just that: "Their engagement with their surroundings is one of the things I both admire and envy about them." He is thinking about the Stegners, who at that time had lived in Los Altos Hills for a good forty years (the entirety of Daniel's life). But after expressing his admiration for staying put, he realistically assesses his and his wife's and most other Americans' condition—"transient, unsettled, passing through." And this is where the genuinely original and enriching philosophy of place begins to emerge in the essay, a respectful departure from the view of Wallace Stegner. Rather than neatly buying into the notion that only a "placed person" can be a whole person, a balanced and happy person, Daniel tries to articulate how a mobile contemporary American can have a meaningful, connected existence. While other cultures and other species have enjoyed the "patterned mobility" of seasonal migration, this is not Daniel's own situation: "My wanderings are separate and random: I am one erratic atom in a field of such atoms, all excited in our various ways by discontent, opportunity, and that sheer restlessness that seems deeply ingrained in the American character."

So how might it be possible to learn the "alphabet of place" when one doesn't stay long enough in any single place to experience its regular rhythms, its long-term patterns? The answer is one of the essential points of environmental literature—it is what Henry David Thoreau once called the "habit of attention." Daniel explains this as follows, his own language becoming so precisely detailed as to embody the very condition of attentiveness he's describing:

> I am learning to pay attention to where I happen to be. I moved to the eastern Oregon ranch at age thirty to see if I could write, and what I found

myself writing about was the stark and singular beauty of the high desert that surrounded me—the dusty stones, the oily smell of sagebrush in hot sun, the coyotes and great horned owls and wind from the rimrock whose voices inhabited the night, the sopping snows and muds of February, the dry shell of summer sky and the gray rumbling buildup to a storm, the rimrock flaring red at sundown as the junipers on the hillside stood out in sharp particularity, each with its long slant shadow.

Vivid details of sensory experience—smells, sounds, sights. So simple and yet so easy to miss in our hustle and bustle. How long must you stay in one place in order "to begin to know where you are and to appreciate it for what it is"? A few years? A few days? Although Daniel proposes here that a residency of a "couple of years" seems requisite, the essay loops toward a concluding discussion of the temporariness of his and Marilyn's stay in Los Altos Hills and implies that belonging to place is a psychological process, not a strictly temporal one. He, like many of his readers, is part of a culture in which mobility "must have a meaning if we are to live and not wither," if we are to support our economic needs and follow our dreams. Like many of his essays, "The Trail Home" concludes elegantly with an instructive narrative, a nighttime scene as John and Marilyn make their way along the path to their cottage, realizing that their feet remember the way home even though their eyes can see little. Although they are living there only temporarily, they "are part of that place, deeply alive and fully present."

Following their stay in the Bay Area, John and Marilyn Daniel lived for several years in Portland, Oregon, before moving to their acre near Elmira. They have now been in the evergreen foothills of the Oregon Coast Range for eight years, and their lives are becoming as deeply rooted there as the Himalayan blackberries, which have also found fertile soil in Oregon's rainy bottomlands and which homeowners like the Daniels must cut back and uproot each year in order to plant tomatoes. But Daniel's recent rootedness does not nullify the powerful import of his concluding argument in "The Trail Home":

> Home for us is not the place we were born, or that perfect somewhere else we used to dream of, but the place where we are—the place we stay long enough to begin to see. It is not a matter of owning the land, or of working the land, but of learning to hold the land in mind, to begin gropingly—blind on a dark hillside—to imagine ourselves as part of it. We know it imperfectly, not mindfully enough. But here we begin, and when we start over in another place we'll take what we know of this place with us, we'll begin this much closer to home.

The concluding lines of this essay display Daniel's characteristic combination of assertiveness and self-deprecation. Admitting his imperfect, insufficiently mindful knowledge of the place where he was living when he wrote the essay, he vows to begin learning the "alphabet of place" in this particular location and to carry this skill, this new language, with him when he moves on. In this final passage of "The Trail Home" we also see the author's unique knack for bringing high-flown abstractions down to earth. This knack is, perhaps, the result of the lyric poet adapting his voice to the form of the essay. Daniel's concern for keeping his language concrete and specific, even when he wants to make a broader argument, is expressed particularly well in the essay "Some Mortal Speculations," a piece that was also collected in the book *The Trail Home.* "My mind, like my hands, is best suited to the grasping of smaller things," he writes, "things that happen close in front of me, things I can see and turn slowly in memory and see again, in imagination's second light." Although this lovely sentence is presented in the first person and seems at first a characteristically humble apology for Daniel's limited ability to process and explain abstract concepts, it actually describes a much more universal human requirement: our shared need for focused sensory details. In a sense, this sentence offers a justification for the very existence of literature and its application to the exploration of issues ranging from philosophy to science and politics.

Readers of *The Trail Home,* resonating to the alphabet-of-place idea and the apparent resignation of the author to a transitory life, might be surprised to read in Daniel's 1996 book, *Looking After: A Son's Memoir,* that the Daniels had moved to—and purchased—a home of their own in 1994. He writes about the move in the epilogue of *Looking After:*

> I stumble loose from our thicket into the neighbor's trees, and as I turn around our new house startles my eyes. I've been glancing out its windows for ten days but have hardly seen *it* in that

time. A plain, brown, slope-roofed, oblong box—
and it's beautiful. It's almost surrounded in Douglas
firs over a hundred feet tall. "We live here," I say
out loud. Today the carpet, tomorrow our furniture and thousand boxes of things. We're out of
the city at last, good city though it was. Maybe,
just maybe, we've finally found our place.

Indeed, the brown house amidst a grove of Douglas
firs seems to reflect a new era of stasis and contentment
in John Daniel's life. However, this does not stop him
from acknowledging and defending the "rootlessness"
and restlessness of American society in general. Initially
published in a 1995 issue of *Orion* magazine, the essay
"A Word in Favor of Rootlessness" has been collected
in revised form in the second edition of *The Norton Book
of Nature Writing,* a forum that will hasten its inclu-
sion in the canon of significant American environmental writing.

One of Daniel's fortes as an essayist is his ability
to bring together lyrical tautness and accessible clarity
of phrasing, combining rich prose style with a broad-
minded reasonableness. The title, "A Word in Favor of
Rootlessness," seems to promise a polemic in support of
rootless wandering, Daniel's erstwhile lifestyle. In fact,
the essay is a reflective, playful piece that considers the
virtues (and pitfalls) of both staying put and hitting the
road. The piece begins by acknowledging the author's
newfound attachment to a specific place on the earth: "I
am one of the converted when it comes to the cultural
and economic necessity of finding place." He sounds
much like his mentor Wallace Stegner when he writes,
"We don't stand much of a chance of perpetuating

115 ☜

ourselves as a culture, or of restoring and sustaining the health of our land, unless we can outgrow our boomer adolescence and mature into stickers, or nesters—human beings willing to take on the obligations of living in communities rooted in place, conserving nature as we conserve ourselves." But this is not the end of the argument. In fact, having initiated a rather staunch perspective on the opening page, Daniel recognizes the merits of the opposite perspective—and he promptly turns around and addresses "some of the less salutary aspects of living in place and some of the joys and perhaps necessary virtues of rootlessness." Nature writing is sometimes assailed in the press as a self-righteous, moralistic genre, but Daniel's tendency in this particular essay and elsewhere to present a complex moral and experiential dilemma that he's wrestling with in his own life certainly counters this worrisome tendency of the genre.

While many "placed writers" celebrate the virtues of identifying with meaningful landscapes over time, Daniel points out that this is not always for the good. He does so by making fun of how the emotional climates of people living in the soggy, gray Pacific Northwest sometimes come to mirror the climate of the place. Blue mood, he jokes, may be an "epiphenomenon of climate." Then, too, there is the tendency of humans, and other animals, to battle over access to and control of places, the result perhaps of "over-identification with place." And what's more, "long-term association with place no more *guarantees* good stewardship than a long-term marriage guarantees a loving and responsible relationship. As Aldo Leopold noted with pain, there are farmers who habitually abuse their land and cannot easily be induced to do otherwise." The essay addresses in stages central tenets of contemporary American environmentalist ethos, considering each issue and with bittersweet ambivalence taking it on and poking holes in deeply held, if uncritical, green codes of belief. He even appreciates anti-environmentalist bumper stickers—HUG A LOGGER—YOU'LL NEVER GO BACK TO TREES—and bemoans the sanctimoniousness of pro-environment slogans such as "Stumps Don't Lie." Sometimes defenders of nature, he laments, can be a humorless lot.

Although Daniel's prose style is in general more reminiscent of the stately, sermonistic style of Wallace Stegner and Wendell Berry, his tendency to deviate from environmental pieties and express antagonistic perspectives is reminiscent of Edward Abbey—and he acknowledges this Abbeyesque impulse in "A Word in Favor of Rootlessness," stating:

> I don't mean to minimize the clear truth that ecological blindness and misconduct are epidemic in our land. I only mean to suggest that rigid ecological correctness may not be the most helpful treatment. All of us, in any place or community or movement, tend to become insiders; we all need the stranger, the outsider, to shake up our perspective and keep us honest. Prominent among Edward Abbey's many virtues was his way of puncturing environmentalist pieties (along with every other brand of piety he encountered).

The true believer, Daniel argues, is akin to the long-time inhabitant of a particular place—both may come to need a new perspective, a broadening encounter with new words, new landscapes, new people. This is probably

117 ☞

a helpful, healthy suggestion for all of us, not only environmentalists but anyone trying to live a constructive civic life. Certainly Stegner and Berry have made strong gestures away from the fold, just as often as they've made the kinds of statements that have raised them to guru status. John Daniel's gentle musings in this essay seem too reasonable to raise any lasting hackles.

Ultimately, his defense of rootlessness comes down to a defense of personal vision. He recalls that one of our greatest wilderness proponents, John Muir, was far less happy as a fruit farmer in Martinez than as a wanderer in the wild Sierras: "Rootedness was not his genius and not his need." Likewise, he recalls how American folk culture, from the songs of Hank Williams to Native American coyote stories, celebrates the traveler, the wanderer, the homeless outsider. Williams's "Ramblin' Man" seems to represent "renewal, vitality, a growing of the soul," while Coyote "fertilizes the locally rooted bloomings of the world." Although the essay concludes by enumerating an assortment of literary wanderers, from Odysseus to Louise Erdrich's Gerry Nanapush, and exalting their contribution to cultural richness, one senses Daniel's own appreciation for the virtues of both settling in and moving on. His own life indicates familiarity with both. The upshot of his writing is that readers must maintain an open, critical mind, adapting to external necessity and private intuition—open to the needs they detect in themselves.

To seek a river's source is to seek our own, to turn and turn and always return—to snow and mountains, to sea and sky, and always to water, always to the soul's

deep springs, always to the flowing ungraspable image
that forever runs free of all names and knowing, sing-
ing the story of its own being, bearing forth from dis-
tant passages its mortal and infinite nature.
—"The Spirit of Rivers"

Much of John Daniel's biography emerges in his literary work, not only in the memoir *Looking After,* but in various essays and essay collections and to some degree in his poetry. The memoir presents concrete details of his family and the idea that the lives of individuals and families are elusive, shifting, and complex, not so easy to describe and explain.

Just as we might be drawn to understand the source of a river, we are compelled to look for the sources of our own imagination, our views of the world—and we want to know, likewise, the sources of an author's words and ideas. Although pinning down these sources can be difficult, here are some of the formal details of Daniel's life, sketched out in more linear fashion than would be available elsewhere. John was born on May 25, 1948, in Spartanburg, South Carolina, to Franz Emil Daniel and Elizabeth ("Zilla") Hawes Daniel. His brother, James Landes Daniel, had been born in Philadelphia three years earlier, in June 1945. Another brother, George Hawes Daniel, had been born in September 1943, but died in Zilla's arms three years later of laryngeal tracheal bronchitis. In a particularly moving section in *Looking After,* the author describes what "Georgie's" death meant to his parents and to himself: "My mother once told me that George was the only human being my father ever loved absolutely, without stay or condition. I love him too, in my own way. I think about him often; I think I might owe my life to him. I carry his picture in my wallet, as if he were not my brother but my son." This episode in the lives of Daniel's parents, which occurred before his own birth, may well have influenced the circumstances of his conception, the tensions between his parents, and much of his own pensive and occasionally somber worldview.

The Daniel family moved quite a bit during John's earlier years, not only in North and South Carolina, but also to Denver, Colorado, for a year, because of Franz's work as an itinerant labor organizer. John explains his parents' backgrounds, social visions, and vocations in the early pages of *Looking After*. His father studied with Reinhold Niebuhr at Union Theological Seminary in New York before shifting his religious zeal to a passion for helping American workers. Zilla was born into a politically moderate and socially proper family in Pennsylvania, the daughter of a Harvard-educated Unitarian minister. She was educated at Kent Place School for Girls in Summit, New Jersey, and at Vassar College, where she became interested in the labor movement. After graduation she worked in a necktie sweatshop and then as a labor activist. It is clear that John's own political awareness and his inevitable linking of the literary/intellectual life with social consciousness flows from a vision of the world inherited from his parents. Likewise, his parents' "rootless, independent lives," determined by the work they had chosen for themselves, were an important influence for many years on John's own way of life.

The Daniels moved to the suburbs of Washington, D.C., in 1954. During this time Zilla and Franz were having difficulties, caused in part by Franz's alcoholism.

Much of this struggle is related in *Looking After*. Eventually, Franz moved out, and John and Jim stayed with Zilla. John saw his father sporadically after moving west to attend college. They never managed to talk to each other about their feelings, although they were at least in occasional communication before Franz's death in 1976. John remained closer with his mother, communicating mostly by letter. Still, despite their gifts of expression, mother and son were incapable of writing about the pain and struggle and confusion they held so deeply in their hearts. John chastises himself in *Looking After:* "And of course it's only now, a year and half past her death, two decades past my father's, that I'm really capable of saying it, and saying it only to a sheet of paper. After running for all those years I double back now when everyone's gone, late as usual, late to my parents' lives and late to my own, I poke and worry through what I can find and make this vessel to hold it." One can derive a good sense of John Daniel's reflective, sensitive nature from the fact that he spent several years in the 1990s, decades after leaving home to attend college, piecing together the details of his own life and his parents' lives, crafting an elegant text of memory that characterizes not only the nuances of his own family but also the tissue of love, frustration, and regret that embodies so many family relationships.

John attended high school in the District of Columbia, while living with his mother. In the fall of 1966, he drove across the country to begin studying at Reed College in Portland, Oregon, having been inspired for years by dreams of the American West and the Pacific Ocean, and especially by the exotic ring of the word

121 ☞

"Oregon." Before finally settling on the title *Looking After* for his memoir, in fact, he used the working title *Toward Oregon* to represent his deep yearning for the state and the thrill its name evoked in him as a young adult. After three semesters at Reed, he found himself preoccupied with drugs, self-exploration, and the mountains, unable to focus on his studies. He left Portland in December 1967 and moved to San Francisco for a year. In 1969, he returned to the Northwest and for the first half of the year worked as a logger in southern Washington, spending his spare time rock climbing and backpacking. During the 1969–70 academic year, he bounced from resumed studies at Reed in the fall to logging in the spring. From 1970 to 1972, he lived in the San Francisco Bay Area, often climbing in Yosemite and backpacking in the Sierra Nevada. Some of the most powerful outdoor experiences of his life occurred during these years, including a climbing experience recorded briefly in his essay "The Impoverishment of Sightseeing" (collected in *The Trail Home*) and more expansively in *Winter Creek*.

But Oregon's persistent pull brought him back north in 1973, and John lived for five years in Klamath Falls, working for the railroad, climbing, backpacking, and beginning to write, first fiction and then poetry. Very little of his fiction has been published, but a rare novella, *The Way of the White Serpent,* was collected in a 1990 volume called *One Step in the Clouds: The Sierra Club Omnibus of Mountaineering Fiction,* edited by Audrey Salkeld and Rosie Smith. In 1978, he moved to a ranch in Langell Valley, east of Klamath Falls. Here he worked as a climbing instructor, a hod carrier, and a poet in the schools. His literary efforts at this time focused on poetry, with some forays into nonfiction. Memories of the Oregon high desert, dating back to the late 1970s and early 1980s, provided vivid imagery for essays that appear in *The Trail Home*. John worked with elementary school children in La Grande, Oregon, in 1980 and 1981 to produce chapbook collections of their poetry, including *The Sun Is Dancing Hot Tonight* (in May 1980) and *Bird, Why Am I Telling These Poems?* (in May 1981). In the years since, John has taught intermittently, mostly at colleges and universities around the country. A small note in his preface to the 1980 student chapbook reflects his pedagogical approach: "In the classroom we aimed not at rhyme schemes or metric arrangements or even 'finished' works, but at something more important—momentary footholds on the slick cliffs of the imagination. Enjoy the poems." The use of creative writing instruction to stimulate students—children or adults—to pay attention to the details of their lives and to think imaginatively about the meaning of these details takes precedence over the mastery of literary forms. In Daniel's own poetry and prose, readers sense his concern for the use of eloquence to explore and exhort, to probe the world, and not merely to exhibit literary prowess.

A major turning point in Daniel's life occurred in 1982 when he was awarded a Wallace Stegner Fellowship in poetry at Stanford University. In addition to attending requisite graduate writing workshops, he took a number of literature courses and accrued enough credits to complete an M.A. in English/Creative Writing at Stanford in 1986, despite the fact that he had never completed his undergraduate degree at Reed. When his Stegner Fellowship ended after one year, John was hired as a

Jones Lecturer in poetry at Stanford, a position he held until 1988. He also served as a lecturer in Freshman English from 1986 to 1988. During his time at Stanford, John benefited from the mentorship and professional examples of such writers as Kenneth Fields, Denise Levertov, and W. S. Di Piero. But perhaps Wallace Stegner was Daniel's greatest influence—an influence that began years earlier when John encountered Stegner's wilderness writings, but became more conscious and intimate when John and his new wife Marilyn Matheson Daniel came to live in a small cottage on the Stegners' property in Los Altos Hills, not far from Stanford, in 1983. Daniel had known Marilyn when he lived near Klamath Falls, where she was a student at the Oregon Institute of Technology. They were married on August 27, 1983, at the ranch in Langell Valley where John lived before coming to Stanford.

After John completed his lectureships at Stanford, he and Marilyn moved to Portland, Oregon, in 1988. Marilyn began working for the Oregon Department of Environmental Quality—where she is now a project manager in the Cleanup Program—while John taught part-time at Lewis & Clark College's Northwest Writing Institute and worked for a book dealer. His first book of poems, *Common Ground,* appeared in the fall of 1988 from Confluence Press, run by James R. Hepworth. As he would recount years later in the preface to the anthology *Wild Song: Poems of the Natural World,* John wrote in 1988 to T. H. ("Tom") Watkins, the editor of *Wilderness* magazine, suggesting that the quarterly publication of the Wilderness Society, one of the nation's largest environmental organizations, should publish poetry in addition to prose. "To my surprise, and perhaps to his," Daniel recalls, "Tom wrote back, 'Why don't we give it a shot? You're the poetry editor.'" John began working as poetry editor for *Wilderness* that very year and continues to this day.

Although he has never held a permanent faculty position, John has served as a writer in residence, a writing workshop instructor, and a visiting lecturer at institutions around the country. In 1991 he spent a semester at Austin Peay State University in Clarksville, Tennessee, followed by stints at Sweet Briar College in Virginia and Ohio State University in 1995 and 1996. He has also worked at the University of Oregon, the University of Montana, and the University of California, Santa Cruz. For the 1997–98 academic year, he was a Research and Writing Fellow at Oregon State University's Center for the Humanities. One of his most important teaching activities has been his role as a guest author at the Art of the Wild summer writing institute, which took place for nearly a decade during the 1990s in Squaw Valley, California, under the auspices of the Creative Writing Program at the University of California, Davis, and the Squaw Valley Community of Writers. Daniel participated in every Art of the Wild gathering but the first, offering public presentations and leading workshops for up-and-coming environmental writers.

The hardcover edition of *The Trail Home* appeared in 1992, followed two years later by an expanded paperback edition, *The Trail Home: Nature, Imagination, and the American West*. Significant uncollected essays, such as "Toward Wild Heartlands," which appeared in the September–October 1994 issue of *Audubon,* have further solidified Daniel's position as an important writer who helps our society imagine its relation to the natural world. In addition to the paperback edition of *The Trail Home,* a new collection of poetry, *All Things Touched By Wind,* came out in 1994.

When John and Marilyn moved to Portland in 1988, their arrival coincided with the recognition that Zilla Daniel, then living on her own in Maine, was no longer capable of managing her affairs, or even her daily needs, without assistance. John helped his mother move to an apartment a short distance from his house in Portland, and within a few months he and Marilyn moved Zilla into their home as her slide into Alzheimer's progressed. The details of their efforts to care for Zilla are braided into the narrative of *Looking After: A Son's Memoir,* which appeared in 1996 from Counterpoint. This memoir combines the story of a son caring for his aging mother and poignant memories of the family's struggles and achievements, and includes Daniel's reflections on his own turbulent process of exploring his life and his relationships. Like *The Trail Home* before it, *Looking After* was awarded an Oregon Book Award for literary nonfiction.

A year after the memoir, John published a very different book in collaboration with photographer Larry N. Olson; *Oregon Rivers* combines the exquisite visual images of a coffee-table photography book with Stegneresque historical and scientific information about rivers throughout the state and the characteristics of flowing water. The impersonal prose represents a significant departure from Daniel's typical literary style, but as

I've suggested, the book's closing meditation, titled "The Spirit of Rivers," is subtly permeated with notions of identity and questions of relationship, sources, and future patterns. A year later, in 1998, the small anthology *Wild Song* was published by the University of Georgia Press, with a brief editorial preface by John. This collection reflects his decade-long efforts as poetry editor of *Wilderness,* and it bears out his remarks in the Nature-Writing Symposium published in the Fall 1992 issue of *Manoa,* in which he asserts that we are experiencing a "green boomlet of poetry" and that "nature prose and poetry are tendrils of the same vine, rooted deeply in our experience of the New World and flourishing today." In addition to producing his own poetry and prose, Daniel has been a significant advocate of contemporary nature poetry in general.

In the fall of 2000, even as he continued to tinker with the manuscript of this *Credo* essay, John embarked on a new project that would lead him to a cabin in the Rogue River backcountry of southwestern Oregon. He spent four and a half months isolated from human news and company, fishing and hunting, growing broccoli, lettuce, and rutabagas, and working on a new manuscript. If *Looking After* focused on his mother, the new project concentrates on charting out the elements of self that come from his father, weaving memory into the narrative of his sojourn in solitude. The book's working title is *River of Solitude: A Winter in the Rogue River Canyon.* This extended stay in the woods—Thanksgiving week till April Fool's Day—resulted in 294 penciled manuscript pages. Like all of John Daniel's work, this book will be difficult to categorize simply as nature writing or memoir, or as an easily recognizable combination of genres. What is more certain is that this forthcoming book, like earlier publications, will demonstrate the inevitable linkages between experience of the natural world and our complex—sometimes tortured—human relationships.

I have mentioned Wallace Stegner several times in this essay, and perhaps it makes sense to pause and consider John Daniel's relationship with Stegner, at least in a glancing fashion. "To seek a river's source is to seek our own"—likewise, to seek the "source" of John Daniel's voice and vision is to seek, to some degree, an understanding of one of the foundational figures in contemporary American environmental literature. Daniel describes his relationship with Stegner in loving, anecdotal detail in the eulogistic essay "Wallace Stegner, 1909–1993," printed in the paperback edition of *The Trail Home* (Stegner died between the publication of the hardcover and paperback editions, from injuries suffered in a New Mexico car accident).

The 1993 essay begins with a lengthy quotation from Stegner's "Wilderness Letter," a defense of wilderness sent in 1960 to a government researcher who was studying the issue of wilderness preservation. Daniel recalls that the letter made its way into the hands of U.S. Secretary of the Interior Stewart Udall, who read the letter aloud as part of a lecture he gave at a conference, a lecture that eventually made its way into a Sierra Club book. Newly arrived from the East, a student at Reed College in Portland, Oregon, Daniel encountered Stegner's words via that Sierra Club collection and was deeply changed. The words "took me by force," he recalls:

I had always been drawn to the outdoors, as a hiker and fisherman back East, and more recently as a climber. And I had always been drawn to words and ideas, the sounds of language, the heft and smells of books. I loved both worlds, but they seemed almost entirely separate.

Now here was a man writing what clearly was literature—writing with measured passion, with gravity and spirit, with knowledge of history, geography, American authors—and nature, wild nature, was his very subject. It was big news to me that a writer could do that.

Stegner's words, and the example of his use of language to explore the relationship between human and natural realms, lodged in Daniel's imagination and stayed with him as he toyed with college for a few years, made his way out into the world to work on the railroad and in the timber business, and then began to try his hand at writing. It was an awestruck young writer who, fresh from the sage and juniper of the high desert in southcentral Oregon, arrived at Stanford University in the fall of 1982, the recipient of a creative writing fellowship named for Stegner—a "bolt from the blue," Daniel has called it. By another lucky turn he and Marilyn spent the next five years living on the Stegners' property as renters and close neighbors. During these years, in the mid-1980s, Daniel's interest in Stegner's writing evolved into a friendship with the man. The two would often talk while working in the garden together.

The essay reminisces fondly about Wallace Stegner as a person and reveals Daniel's personal relationship with him. Several years later, for Curt Meine's book *Wallace Stegner and the Continental Vision: Essays on Literature,*

History, and Landscape, Daniel wrote an elegant commentary on Stegner's literary and environmental vision called "Wallace Stegner's Hunger for Wholeness" that more formally addresses the goals and strategies of Stegner's writing. As is often the case when the literary artist turns to critical analysis, the comments reveal as much about the speaker as they do about the subject. Several of the passages from this essay are helpful in appreciating John Daniel's own concerns and strategies. First, after applauding the broad range of Stegner's experimentation in various prose genres (the novel, the short story, the essay, memoir, history, biography, literary journalism), Daniel considers his mentor's gestures toward poetry and the possible reasons for Stegner's sticking with prose in his well-known published work. After quoting three paragraphs from Stegner's essay "Overture: The Sound of Mountain Water," Daniel writes:

> If I had camped by that river and written a short essay about it, I wouldn't have included the preliminary details of the river's history because I wouldn't have known them and wouldn't have looked them up. I might have mentioned the Continental Divide but probably not the source and length and terminus of the river—again, I wouldn't have known or sought that information. In short, I would have written, whether in prose or in verse, a lyric poem about my first encounter with a mountain river. And maybe that suggests one reason why Wallace Stegner didn't write verse. For the poet—if I may overgeneralize to make a point—the lyric moment is consuming and aesthetically sufficient unto itself. For Stegner, the lyric moment may be intense but is never in itself

aesthetically sufficient. In his nonfiction you will find lyrical passages of exquisite grace, but you will not find personal rhapsody without a context of geography and history. For Wallace Stegner, the merely personal is not the stuff of which literature is made.

Although these comments are written with obvious respect for Stegner's work, they also illustrate a key difference between Daniel and Stegner. For Daniel, a lyric poet before he became an essayist, the intensity of the "lyric moment" has at times been a primary goal. Likewise, even in his essays, Daniel clearly depends upon and celebrates the richness of personal experience, producing resonant personal anecdotes from which he then spins larger philosophical, psychological, ecological, and sometimes political messages. While Stegner often felt drawn, fundamentally, to the impersonal context of his topics, Daniel typically begins with personal experience and makes the most of emotional episodes, not stopping with self-exploration and self-revelation, but nonetheless using the self as a point of departure.

Daniel is clearly fascinated by Stegner's sense of the insufficiency of the merely personal. He enlarges his point by discussing Stegner's memoir *Wolf Willow*, an account of growing up on the remote western plains of Canada, noting how the book begins with a brief sentence about the self—"It is the place where I spent my childhood"—sandwiched between two longer sentences about the cultural and geophysical characteristics of the place. Daniel's own literary work implies that we are missing some crucial aspect of our lives as human animals if we fail to accept, if we fail to celebrate, our

131 ☙

physical senses and our use of the senses to engage with the planet. Much of his writing examines and enacts the experience of going through the world alert to both sensation and the implications of what we perceive.

I can think, for example, of one of Daniel's poems that offers a particularly sharp contrast to Stegner's relatively selfless style of presenting personal experience. This poem appears in each of Daniel's two books of poetry, *Common Ground* (1988) and *All Things Touched By Wind* (1994). It is the only poem reprinted from the first book in the second. In *Common Ground,* the piece is titled "At Thirty-Five." In the more recent collection, it is presented as section one (of twelve) in a series called "The Unseen." The poem itself is unchanged:

> Mustard crowds the barbed-wire fence,
> the entire hillside thick with light
> and glowing brighter as the pale sky
> goes dim. The single oak is hazed
> with April leaves. Across the valley
> children call, quick strokes of sound.
> A wavering cloud of sparrows passes,
> a kestrel hovers on beating wings—
> impossibly much, but I need more tonight
> than the bare glory of what's given.
> I need to rub this moment in mind
> for the shimmer of meaning I almost see,
> I need the boy who stood shivering once
> in a different field, hands clenched
> at his sides in the clammy dusk
> as he silently burned into mind
> the whippoorwills, silhouettes of trees,
> the bright clear blue of the west—
> *I'll remember,* he whispered, *even
> when I'm dead I'll remember this.*

The poem evokes the ultimate Wordsworthian "spot of time," a moment of sensory experience that "shimmers" with almost perceived "meaning"—movement and stillness, sound and silence, collapsing together as revelation of the self's genuine presence in the world. Human beings seem to forget all too easily that we exist in a world of relationships, with our own kind and with many other beings. It comes to us as an inevitable revelation that we are not alone and that there is possibly meaning enough in this experience of engagement with the world beyond our specific bodies. "I need to rub this moment in mind," writes the poet, recalling an earlier boyhood self who sought to "burn into mind" a similar moment of awareness. Remember, remember, remember—pay attention and remember. This is the implied exhortation to the writer himself and to his reader. It seems quite possible that Wallace Stegner would find this process self-indulgent and wanting. But Daniel has his own agenda as a writer, and it does not merely mirror that of his mentor.

It is quite possible that the seeker of memorable sensations could find himself content with private, insular hedonism—loving only the self and the self's alertness to the world. One of the significant features of John Daniel's work, however, is its sensitivity to the importance of relationships. When Daniel came to write *Looking After: A Son's Memoir* in the early 1990s, he produced a book vastly different from Stegner's *Wolf Willow,* offering powerful insight into the process of self-examination and into a wonderfully complex mother-son relationship. Geography and history are present in Daniel's story, but the foregrounded narrative is one of

133

personal journey and the process of "looking after." The book's forty chapters, packaged between a prologue and an epilogue, alternate between essays about the author's own process of moving to the West and learning to weather his fluctuations of mood and essays about his aging mother's arrival in Portland to live with John and Marilyn during her final four years of life.

Perhaps the deepest "environmental" dimension of *Looking After* is in the representation of John's relationship with his mother, Zilla, a strikingly independent and uncompromising woman, even into her seventies. The book is full of tenderness and remorse and full of darker emotions such as impatience and frustration as Zilla fell deeper and deeper into the helplessness of Alzheimer's, and her son and daughter-in-law became increasingly responsible for her every need. But what emerges in the narrative, at least in my reading of it, is the awesome, positive potential for people—men and women—to "look after" what they love, to care about another person's life enough to remember it and prepare the kind of written document we call "memoir" and to care enough to tend to the most banal and awkward requirements of daily life. One of my favorite passages in the book is an odd little segment about John's experience helping his mother take a shower. Here is the last part of that story:

> I helped my mother down into a straight-backed chair and left her in the bathroom with towels, clean underwear, and a little space heater to keep her warm. She took her time, as with everything. Often it was half an hour before she emerged in her dressing gown, her hair beginning to fluff,

her face smiling. No matter how hard she might have resisted the idea, a bath or shower always seemed to renew her. Soap or no soap, the old woman came forth cleaner of spirit.

"She was pure as the driven snow," she usually quoted, gaily, then a pause: "But she drifted."

I guess I came out of the bathroom cleaner of spirit myself. Soap or no soap, whatever the tenor of our conversation, I appreciate now what a privilege it was to help my mother with her shower. I wish I'd seen it more clearly at the time. We don't get to choose our privileges, and the ones that come to us aren't always the ones we would choose, and each of them is as much burden as joy. But they do come, and it's important to know them for what they are.

John Daniel wrote this book as a form of tribute to his mother and as a way of thinking through his own quest for a comfortable understanding of personal identity—it's not always a pretty self-portrait, but it's not maudlin or pettily self-deprecating, either. It feels candid, and the abiding emotion is tenderness—and this from a towering ex-logger and rock climber. I regard the care-giving stories of *Looking After* as beautiful examples of how the work of a so-called "nature writer" is as deeply engaged with human relationships as it is with the more-than-human world.

I have known John Daniel since I was a twenty-two-year-old college senior and he was a Stegner Fellow at Stanford, newly returned to academia after years of back-packing and cliff climbing, doing manual labor in the forests and train yards of the West, and undertaking a solitary effort to develop his literary voice. John walked into a lecture hall in Stanford's outer Quad in September 1982 to attend Lawrence V. Ryan's course on English Renaissance literature wearing, as I recall, cutoff jeans and high-top basketball shoes. I can't recall the poet-scholar, who was thirty-four at the time, wearing anything else that year, not even when giving a public reading of his work. In those days, John was still unsettled and itinerant, even in his choice of vocation. We didn't talk about environmental literature or environmental issues—my own work was not yet moving in that direction, either.

I find myself gazing now at a series of photographs I took of John in the summer of 1998 in the backyard of his home. He is hamming for the camera, playfully posing—in one shot he is relaxing in a hammock beneath giant Douglas firs, smiling, hands behind his head. In another, he is reading aloud while sitting, fully clothed in jeans and t-shirt, in an antique bathtub on the back porch. These are images of warmth and contentment, showing one of the most capable American writers at a new plateau of restfulness in his life. As *Winter Creek* and the evolving manuscript of *River of Solitude* demonstrate, this restfulness has not resulted in a stillness of the imagination, but rather in a secure platform for developing new explorations of self and world.

Bibliography of John Daniel's Work

By James S. Guignard Jr.

BOOKS

With Larry N. Olson. *Oregon Rivers*. Englewood, Colo.: Westcliffe Publishers, 1997.

Looking After: A Son's Memoir. Washington, D.C.: Counterpoint Press, 1996.

All Things Touched by Wind. Anchorage: Salmon Run Press, 1994.

The Trail Home. New York: Pantheon Books, 1992.

Common Ground. Lewiston, Idaho: Confluence Press, 1988.

EDITED BOOKS

Wild Song: Poems of the Natural World. Athens: University of Georgia Press, 1998.

UNCOLLECTED JOURNAL, MAGAZINE, AND NEWSPAPER PUBLICATIONS

"The Flow of Life." *Audubon* 104, no. 1 (January/February 2002): 47–48.

"The Prankster Moves On: Remembering Ken Kesey." *Open Spaces* 4, no. 3 (Winter 2001–2002): 8–11.

"Terrorism Shouldn't Push Us to Judicial Extremes." *West Lane News* (December 13, 2001): 6.

"In the Matter of Clear-cutting, the Vision Is Less Clear."
West Lane News (September 13, 2001): 7.

"Our Experimental Hermit Weighs His Sojourn." *West Lane News* (July 7, 2001): 6.

"A Fertile Meadow Far from Town." *Open Spaces* 3, no. 4 (Winter 2000).

"Strategic Retreat: A Writer Samples Solitude." *West Lane News* (November 30, 2000): 6.

Excerpts from "Homing In on Oregon." *Open Spaces* 3, no. 3 (Summer 2000).

"Toward Oregon: A Writer's Natural History." *Writing Nature* (Summer 2000): 1–4.

"Tally a Write-in for Polling-Place Inconvenience." *West Lane News* (June 22, 2000): 2.

"The Province of the Personal Narrative." *Weber Studies* 16, no. 2 (Winter 1999): 8–17.

"Seeing With Both Eyes." *Connotations: The Island Institute Journal* (Summer 1998).

"Winter Creek." *Open Spaces* 1, no. 3 (Summer 1998): 10–11.

"Writing in the West." *Open Spaces* 1, no. 2 (Spring 1998).

"Fading Promise." *Audubon* 99, no. 6 (November/December 1997): 76.

"The Totem." *Outside* 22, no. 10 (October 1997): 91.

"Wallace Stegner's Hunger for Wholeness." *High Plains Literary Review* (Fall 1997): 32–47.

"Boulder Dance." *Appalachia* 51, no. 2 (December 1996).

"Homing In on Oregon." *Eugene Weekly* (December 14, 1995).

"Washington: Holding Their Own in the Okanogan." *Wilderness* 59, no. 211 (Winter 1995): 19–21.

"Beauty of the Wild." *Resurgence,* no. 173 (November/December 1995).

"A Word in Favor of Rootlessness." *Orion* 14, no. 4 (Autumn 1995): 34–37.

"Dutch Henry Journal." *Writing Nature* (Summer 1995).

"Toward Wild Heartlands." *Audubon* 96, no. 5 (September/ October 1994): 38.

"Wallace Stegner: A Remembrance." *Bloomsbury Review* 14, no. 4 (July/August 1994): 9.

"The Limits of Paradise." *Sierra* 79, no. 2 (March/April 1994): 64–72, 142–43.

"The Trail Home." *Folio A* 2 (Fall 1993): 100–111. (Translated into Japanese in a special American nature writing issue, edited by Ken-ichi Noda and Scott Slovic.)

"William Stafford, 1914–1993." *Western American Literature* 28, no. 3 (Fall 1993): 231.

"Cuttings." *Summit* 34, no. 2 (Summer 1993).

"A Chance to Do It Right." *Wilderness* 56, no. 201 (Summer 1993): 10–33.

"Writing Nature." *American Nature Writing Newsletter* 5, no. 1 (Spring 1993).

"Dance of Denial." *Sierra* 78, no. 2 (March/April 1993): 64–73.

"The Rise of Nature Writing: America's Next Great Genre?" *Manoa* 4, no. 2 (Fall 1992): 73–96. (One of many contributions to a nature writing symposium.)

"Turnings of Seasons." *Sierra* 77, no. 1 (January/February 1992): 22–23.

"Old Growth on the Dry Side." *High Country News* 22, no. 22 (November 19, 1990): 27–28.

"Stealing Time." *Wilderness* 53, no. 188 (Spring 1990): 18.

"The Canadian Cut." *Wilderness* 52, no. 182 (Fall 1988): 61.

"The Long Dance of the Trees." *Wilderness* 51, no. 180 (Spring 1988): 18.

"Water Power." *Wilderness* 50, no. 175 (Winter 1986): 54–55.

Review of *E. T.—The Extra-Terrestial* directed by Steven Spielberg. *Klamath Falls Herald and News* (July 23, 1982).

"Uprising, or The Downing of Turnips." *Climbing,* no. 63 (November/December 1980): 30–35.

"The Trojan Nuclear Plant: The Politics of Occupation." *Mountain Gazette* 76/7 (December 1978/January 1979).

"The Fall." *Climbing,* no. 45 (November/December 1977).

BOOK REVIEWS BY JOHN DANIEL

"A Writer for All Seasons." Review of *Wallace Stegner: His Life and Work,* by Jackson L. Benson. *Portland Oregonian* (November 24, 1996).

Review of *The River of the Mother of God and Other Essays by Aldo Leopold,* edited by Susan L. Flader and J. Baird Callicott. *Western Historical Quarterly* 23, no. 3 (Summer 1992): 402.

Review of *We Animals: Poems of Our World,* edited by Nadya Aisenberg. *Orion Nature Quarterly* 9, no. 2 (Spring 1990): 56–58.

Review of *Under the Sign of the Neon Wolf* by Paulann Peterson. *Calapooya Collage* (Summer 1989).

UNCOLLECTED POEMS

"The Wind in Sand Creek Canyon." *Bloomsbury Review* (July/August 2000).

"The Canyon." *Metre: A Magazine of International Poetry,* no. 7/8 (Spring/Summer 2000): 242–46.

"Poem for Fern Ridge Library." *Reed: A Quarterly Magazine of Personalities, Actions, and Ideas* 79, no. 2 (May 2000): 37.

"The Canyon." *ISLE: Interdisciplinary Studies in Literature and Environment* 4, no. 1 (Spring 1997): 107–8.

"Spring Burning." *Texas Observer* (1995).

"Ourselves" and "Coyote Bloodsong." *South Dakota Review* 23, no. 1 (Spring 1985): 52–53.

"Report to the Snail Darter." *Not Man Apart* 9, no. 12 (November 1979).

BOOK FOREWORDS/AFTERWORDS

"Homing In on Oregon." In *Oregon Then and Now,* by Benjamin Gifford and Steve Terrill. Englewood, Colo.: Westcliffe Publishers, 2000.

Oregon: Magnificent Wilderness, by Steve Terrill. Englewood, Colo.: Westcliffe Publishers, 1991.

ANTHOLOGY APPEARANCES—ESSAYS

"A Word In Favor of Rootlessness." In *The Norton Book of Nature Writing,* edited by Robert Finch and John Elder, 983–90. New York: W. W. Norton, 2002. Also appears the trade edition of this anthology, titled *Nature Writing: The Tradition in English.*

"Swimming Among the Ruins." In *Oregon Salmon: Essays on the State of the Fish at the Turn of the Millennium,* compiled by Oregon Trout, 7–10. Portland: Oregon Trout, 2001.

"My Mother at the End of Her Life." In *Signs of Hope: In Praise of Ordinary Heroes,* edited by Jon Wilson and Kimberly Ridley, 233–40. Wainscott, N.Y.: Pushcart Press, 2000.

"A Word in Favor of Rootlessness." In *Literature and the Environment: A Reader on Nature and Culture,* edited by Lorraine Anderson, Scott Slovic, and John P. O'Grady, 259–63. New York: Longman, 1999.

"Waist Deep in Blackberry Vines." In *American Nature Writing 1998,* edited by John A. Murray, 123–28. San Francisco: Sierra Club Books, 1998.

"Boulder Dance." In *The Height of Our Mountains: Nature Writing from Virginia's Blue Ridge Mountains and Shenandoah Valley,* edited by Michael P. Branch and Daniel J. Philippon, 342–45. Baltimore: Johns Hopkins University Press, 1998.

"Desert Walking." In *Natural State: A Literary Anthology of California Nature Writing,* edited by Steven Gilbar, 189–99. Berkeley: University of California Press, 1998.

Excerpts from "The Impoverishment of Sightseeing," "Among Animals," and "The Beauty of the Wild." In *The Sacred Earth: Writers on Nature and Spirit,* edited by

Jason Gardner, 7, 37, 117, 134. Novato, Calif.: New
World Library, 1998.

"Wallace Stegner's Hunger for Wholeness." In *Wallace
Stegner and the Continental Vision,* edited by Curt Meine,
31–42. Washington, D.C.: Island Press, 1997.

"The Cultivated Wild of Wallace Stegner." In *Catching the
Light: Remembering Wallace Stegner,* edited by Page Stegner
and Mary Stegner, 24–30. Stanford, Calif.: Stanford
University Library, 1996.

"Turnings of Seasons." In *The Earth at Our Doorstep: Contemporary Writers Celebrate the Landscapes of Home,* edited
by Annie Stine, 39–45. San Francisco: Sierra Club Books,
1996.

"A Word in Favor of Rootlessness." In *Facing the Lion:
Writers on Life and Craft,* edited by Kurt Brown, 131–37.
Boston: Beacon Press, 1996.

"The Cultivated Wild of Wallace Stegner." In *The Geography
of Hope,* edited by Page Stegner and Mary Stegner, 75–82.
San Francisco: Sierra Club Books, 1996.

"The Beauty of the Wild." In *The Soul Unearthed,* edited
by Cass Adams, 183–85. New York: G. P. Putnam's Sons,
1996.

"Cuttings." In *American Nature Writing 1995,* edited by
John A. Murray, 238–45. San Francisco: Sierra Club
Books, 1995.

"The Long Dance of the Trees." In *The World of Wilderness:
Essays on the Power and Purpose of Wild Country,* edited by
T. H. Watkins and Patricia Byrnes, 153–69. Niwot, Colo.:
Roberts Rinehart, 1995.

"Cuttings." In *Northern Lights,* edited by Deborah Clow
and Donald Snow, 203–6. New York: Vintage, 1994.

Excerpt from "The Impoverishment of Sightseeing." In
The West: A Treasury of Art and Literature, edited by T. H.
Watkins and Joan Watkins, 346–48. New York: Hugh
Lauter Levin Associates, 1994.

"Some Mortal Speculations" and "The Impoverishment of

Sightseeing." In *Being in the World: An Environmental Reader for Writers,* edited by Scott H. Slovic and Terrell F. Dixon, 84–89, 592–98. New York: Macmillan, 1993.

"Cuttings." In *Beloved of the Sky,* edited by John Ellison, 69–75. Seattle: Broken Moon Press, 1992.

"The Impoverishment of Sightseeing." In *Nature's New Voices,* edited by John A. Murray, 146–54. Golden, Colo.: Fulcrum Publishing, 1992.

ANTHOLOGY APPEARANCES—POEMS AND FICTION

"The Canyon" and "The Canyon Wren." In *Getting Over the Color Green: Contemporary Environmental Literature of the Southwest,* edited by Scott Slovic, 15–18. Tucson: University of Arizona Press, 2001.

"Sucked in the raft and spat us out." In *The Great Oregon Serial Poem,* edited by Jack Lorts, 21. Talent, Oreg.: Talent House Press, 2001.

"Spring Burning." In *Wild Song: Poems of the Natural World,* edited by John Daniel, 17. Athens: University of Georgia Press, 1998.

"Moment" and "To Mt. St. Helens." In *Poetry of the American West,* edited by Alison Hawthorne Deming, 269–72. New York: Columbia University Press, 1996.

"In Praise." In *The Soul Unearthed,* edited by Cass Adams, 10–11. New York: G. P. Putnam's Sons, 1996.

"I came home to the bean vines." In *Crestone Chapbook,* edited by J. Parker Huber. Brattleboro, Vt.: J. Parker Huber, 1995.

"Naming the New One." In *Northern Lights,* edited by Deborah Clow and Donald Snow, 79–80. New York: Vintage, 1994.

"In Praise." In *Poems for the Wild Earth,* edited by Gary Lawless. Nobelboro, Maine: Blackberry Books, 1994.

"Dependence Day." In *From Here We Speak: An Anthology*

of Oregon Poetry, edited by Ingrid Wendt and Primus
St. John, 190. Corvallis: Oregon State University Press,
1993.

"Common Ground" and "The Unborn of the Nuclear
Age." In *The Forgotten Language: Contemporary Poets and
Nature,* edited by Christopher Merrill, 34–35. Salt Lake
City: Peregrine Smith Books, 1991.

"To William Stafford." In *Stafford's Road: An Anthology of
Poems for William Stafford,* edited by Thomas L. Ferte, 38.
Monmouth, Oreg.: Adrienne Lee Press, 1991.

"The Way of the White Serpent." In *One Step in the Clouds:
An Omnibus of Mountaineering Novels and Short Stories,*
edited by Audrey Salkeld and Rosie Smith, 205–18.
London: Diadem, 1990.

"Return." In *Poetry from the Amicus Journal,* edited by Peter
Borrelli and Brian Swann, 14. Palo Alto, Calif.: Tioga
Publishing, 1990.

"Of Earth" and "A Year Among the Owls." In *The Uncommon
Touch: Fiction and Poetry from the Stanford Writing Work-
shop,* edited by John L'Heureux, 89–92. Stanford, Calif.:
Stanford Alumni Association, 1989.

"Fort Barry" and "The Burden." In *The Beast in a Cage of
Words,* edited by Alan Cohen, 4, 18–19. Chester, Mass.:
Sun's Nest Press, 1985.

"The Longing." In *The Pushcart Prize VIII: Best of the Small
Presses,* edited by Bill Henderson, 345–46. Wainscott,
N.Y.: Pushcart Press, 1983.

"The Way of the White Serpent." In *Ascent: The Mountaineering Experience in Word and Image,* edited by Allen
Steck and Steve Roper. San Francisco: Sierra Club Books,
1980.

"Forts," "Notes to a Young Fisherman," and "Christmas in
the Oregon County, 1829." In *Third Season/Seven Poets,*
edited by Sandra Gullickson. La Grande, Oreg.: Clear-
water Press, 1980.

VIDEO RECORDINGS

"Art of the Wild." Foundation for Global Community, 1996. (Foundation for Global Community; 800-707-7932.)

"A Tribute to Wallace Stegner." Schoenfeldt Distinguished Writers Series, 1993. (University of Portland Magazine; 503-943-7202.)

"Ancient Forests: Vanishing Legacy of the Pacific Northwest." Wilderness Society, 1989. (Wilderness Society; 202-429-2612.)

"Wilderness and the Imagination." U.S. Forest Service—Pacific Southwest Region, 1989. (Forest Service Video Library; 800-683-8366)

PUBLIC ART

"Read then, if you will." Interior frieze created for Fern Ridge Library, Veneta, Oreg., September 1999.

INTERVIEWS

Jim Burch. "A Conversation with John Daniel." *Timeline*, no. 22 (July/August 1995): 6–9.

Wendy Madar. "Union Organizer, Drinker, Father: A Son Looks for the Truth." *Center for the Humanities Newsletter* (Fall 1997): 1, 6, 8.

BIOGRAPHICAL/CRITICAL STUDIES AND BOOK REVIEWS

Anderson, Lorraine. "New Voices in American Nature Writing." *American Nature Writers*. Vol. 2, edited by John Elder. New York: Scribner's, 1996.

Baker, Jeff. Review of *Oregon Rivers*. *Portland Oregonian* (December 28, 1997).

Barnard, Jeff. "Winter in the Woods Rejuvenates Writer." *Eugene Register-Guard* (June 2, 2001).

———. "Remote Rogue Homestead a Haven for Writers." *Eugene Register-Guard* (June 5, 1994).

———. "High Desert Landscape Exhilirates Poet's Heart." *Grants Pass Daily Courier* (August 21, 1989).

Brown, Kathy. "When the Golden Years Lose Their Luster." *Lexington Herald-Leader* (December 8, 1996).

Bryson, J. Scott. Review of *Wild Song*. *ISLE: Interdisciplinary Studies in Literature and Environment* 6, no. 2 (Summer 1999): 224–25.

Bucharest, Susan. Review of *Wild Song*. *Open Spaces* 1, no. 3 (Summer 1998).

Butler, Robert Olen. "Enchanted, Lyric Essays from the Natural World." *Chicago Tribune Books* (August 2, 1992).

Cassell, Faris. Review of *Wild Song*. *Eugene Register-Guard* (July 12, 1998).

———. Review of *Oregon Rivers*. *Eugene Register-Guard* (November 2, 1997).

———. Review of *Looking After*. *Eugene Register-Guard* (October 27, 1996).

Crittenden, Lindsey. Review of *Looking After*. *Berkeley Express* (January 31, 1997).

Dixon, Jim. "Liquid Assets." *Willamette Week* (September 10, 1997).

———. "Northern Exposure." *Willamette Week* (June 18, 1992).

Dixon, Terrell. "Three Examples of New Nature Writing." *American Nature Writing Newsletter* 5 (Spring 1993).

Dye, John. Review of *Looking After*. *Library Journal* 122, no. 8 (October 1, 1996).

Graham, Renee. "Age Reverses Role for a Mother and Son." *Boston Globe* (October 24, 1996).

Gwartney, Debra. "Mother and Child." *Eugene Weekly* (December 26, 1996).

Hanson, Susan. Review of *Wild Song*. *San Marcos Daily Record* (July 12, 1998).

————. Review of *The Trail Home*. *San Marcos Daily Record* (August 5, 1992).

Hays, Don. "Books Celebrate Richness of Oregon's Outdoor Life." *Salem Statesman-Journal* (September 28, 1997).

Jameson, Sara. Review of *Oregon Rivers*. *Grants Pass Daily Courier* (October 23, 1997).

————. Review of *The Trail Home*. *Riverside Press-Enterprise* (August 23, 1992).

"John Daniel '70: A Poem for a Library." *Reed: A Quarterly Magazine of Personalities, Actions, and Ideas* 79, no. 2 (May 2000): 37.

Johnson, David. Review of *Wild Song*. *Eugene Weekly* (July 2, 1998).

Juillerat, Lee. Review of *Looking After*. *Klamath Falls Herald and News* (October 17, 1996).

————. "Klamath Basin Excited Him 'in a Writerly Way.'" *Klamath Falls Herald and News* (March 16, 1989).

Laing, David. "*Common Ground* by John Daniel: An Appreciation." *Fireweed* (July 1990).

Little, Charles E. "Books for the Wilderness." *Wilderness* 56, no. 198 (Fall 1992).

Lucas, Susan. Review of *Looking After*. *ISLE: Interdisciplinary Studies in Literature and Environment* 5, no. 2 (Summer 1998): 144–45.

Marx, Doug. "Brilliant Local Poets Fix on Nature As Their True North(west)." Review of *All Things Touched By Wind*. *Portland Oregonian* (February 5, 1995).

Memmott, David. Review of *Common Ground*. *Ice River* (Fall 1998).

Muller, Erik. Review of *All Things Touched By Wind*. *Fireweed* (Spring 1995).

Murray, John. Review of *Looking After*. *Bloomsbury Review* 17, no. 2 (March/April 1997).

Pahmeier, Gailmarie. Review of *Common Ground*. *Redneck Review* 16 (Spring 1989).

Petty, Connie. "Oregon Rivers." *Albany Democrat-Herald* (January 14, 1998).

Pintarich, Paul. Review of *The Trail Home*. *Portland Oregonian* (June 28, 1992).

Rawlins, C. L. Review of *Common Ground*. *Calapooya Collage* (Summer 1989).

Review of *Wild Song*. *Baton Rouge Advocate* (July 26, 1998).

Review of *Looking After*. *Washington Post* (January 5, 1997).

Review of *Looking After*. *Publishers Weekly* 243, no. 37 (September 9, 1996).

Review of *The Trail Home*. *Guardian Weekly* 147 (September 27, 1992).

Review of *The Trail Home*. *Washington Post Book World* 22 (July 5, 1992).

Review of *The Trail Home*. *Audubon* 94, no. 3 (Summer 1992).

Review of *The Trail Home*. *Library Journal* 117 (June 15, 1992).

Review of *The Trail Home*. *Publishers Weekly* 239, no. 22 (May 11, 1992).

Review of *The Trail Home*. *Kirkus Reviews* 60 (April 15, 1992).

Review of *Common Ground*. *Publishers Weekly* 234 (July 22, 1988).

Salm, Arthur. Review of *The Trail Home*. *San Diego Union-Tribune* (August 9, 1992).

Schaeffer, Danna Wilner. "Healing Death's Sting." *Portland Oregonian* (January 9, 1997).

Schneider, Bart. "Life with Mother." *Newsday* (February 9, 1997).

Siporin, Ona. Review of *Common Ground*. *Western American Literature* 24, no. 3 (Fall 1989).

Skloot, Floyd. "Piecing Together Memory's Shards." *Portland Oregonian* (October 13, 1996).

———. Review of *The Trail Home*. *Northwest Review* 31, no. 1 (1993).

Slovic, Scott. Review of *The Trail Home*. *Western American Literature* 28, no. 1 (Spring 1993).

Wendt, Ingrid. Review of *All Things Touched By Wind*. *Western American Literature* 30, no. 1 (Spring 1995).

Wittman, Juliet. "On Death and Dying." *Washington Post* (March 16, 1997).

ACKNOWLEDGMENTS FOR "WINTER CREEK"

by John Daniel

For help of various kinds in the preparation of this book I am grateful to Jeff Cramer, Victor Friedman, John Laursen, David Robinson, Bill Rossi, Scott Slovic, Mary Page Stegner, and especially my wife, Marilyn Matheson Daniel.

The first two sections of the final chapter appeared previously in *Oregon Quarterly* as "The Untellable Story." Certain other streaks and passages of the text appeared previously, in different form, in *Appalachia, Open Spaces, Resurgence, Sierra, Summit, West Lane News,* and *Writing Nature,* and in these books:

The Earth at Our Doorstep: Contemporary Writers Celebrate the Landscapes of Home, edited by Annie Stine (Sierra Club Books, 1996).

The Height of Our Mountains: Nature Writing from Virginia's Blue Ridge Mountains and Shenandoah Valley, edited by Michael P. Branch and Daniel J. Philippon (Johns Hopkins University Press, 1998).

Oregon Then and Now, by Benjamin Gifford and Steve Terrill (Westcliffe Publishers, 2000).

The Soul Unearthed: Celebrating Wildness and Personal Renewal through Nature, edited by Cass Adams (G. P. Putnam's Sons, 1996).

I thank the editors and publishers of all.

WORKS CITED

p. 8   Dylan Thomas, "Fern Hill," in *The Collected Poems of Dylan Thomas 1934–1952* (New York: New Directions, 1971), 178.

p. 8   e. e. cummings, "65," in *Complete Poems 1913–1962* (New York: Harcourt Brace Jovanovich, 1972), 663.

p. 21   Walt Whitman, "Beginning My Studies," in *Walt Whitman: Complete Poetry and Collected Prose* (New York: Library of America, 1982), 171.

p. 40   Gary Snyder, "Piute Creek," in *Riprap and Cold Mountain Poems* (San Francisco: Grey Fox Press, 1980), 6.

p. 56   William Stafford, "Vocation," in *Stories That Could Be True: New and Collected Poems* (New York: Harper and Row, 1977), 107.

p. 60   Wendell Berry, "The Old Elm Tree by the River," in *The Country of Marriage* (New York: Harcourt Brace Jovanovich, 1973), 3.

p. 89   Loren Eiseley, *The Immense Journey* (New York: Random House, 1957), 8.

p. 89   Eiseley, *The Immense Journey,* 10.

p. 90   Emily Dickinson, "The earth has many keys,"
in *The Complete Poems of Emily Dickinson,* ed.
Thomas H. Johnson (Boston: Little, Brown and
Company, 1960), 716.

p. 91   Charles Darwin, *On the Origin of Species* (New
York: D. Appleton, 1881), 429.

p. 92   Eiseley, *The Immense Journey,* 26.

p. 92   C. G. Jung, *Answer to Job,* trans. R. F. C. Hull
(London: Routledge and Kegan Paul, 1954), 96.

p. 94   Henry David Thoreau, *The Maine Woods* (Boston: Riverside Press, 1889), 71.

p. 96   A. R. Ammons, "Poetics," in *Collected Poems
1951–1971* (New York: W. W. Norton, 1972),
191.

p. 96–97 Ralph Waldo Emerson, "The Poet," in *Essays:
Second Series* (Boston: James Munroe, 1844), 10.

p. 102   Dickinson, "What mystery pervades a well!"
in *The Complete Poems of Emily Dickinson,*
599–600.

p. 105   John Daniel, "The Spirit of Rivers." in *Oregon
Rivers,* photos by Larry N. Olson (Englewood,
Colo.: Englewood Publishers, 1997), 159.

p. 107   Wallace Stegner, "The Sense of Place," in *Where
the Bluebird Sings to the Lemonade Springs: Living
and Writing in the West* (New York: Random
House, 1992), 199.

p. 107   Stegner, *Where the Bluebird Sings,* 205.

p. 108   Stegner, *Where the Bluebird Sings,* 206.

p. 108   Stegner, *Where the Bluebird Sings,* 205.

p. 108   Daniel, "The Trail Home," in *The Trail Home* (New York: Pantheon Books, 1992), 203.

p. 108   Daniel, *The Trail Home,* 203.

p. 108   Daniel, *The Trail Home,* 205.

p. 109   Daniel, *The Trail Home,* 205.

p. 109–10   Daniel, *The Trail Home,* 205–6.

p. 110   Daniel, *The Trail Home,* 206.

p. 110   Daniel, *The Trail Home,* 206.

p. 110–11   Daniel, *The Trail Home,* 206.

p. 111   Daniel, *The Trail Home,* 207.

p. 111   Daniel, *The Trail Home,* 208.

p. 111   Thoreau, *The Journal of Henry David Thoreau,* vol. 4, ed. Bradford Torrey and Francis H. Allen (Boston: Houghton Mifflin, 1906), 351.

p. 111–12   Daniel, *The Trail Home,* 208–9.

p. 112   Daniel, *The Trail Home,* 209.

p. 112   Daniel, *The Trail Home,* 209.

p. 112   Daniel, *The Trail Home,* 212.

p. 112   Daniel, *The Trail Home,* 212.

p. 113   Daniel, *The Trail Home,* 212–13.

p. 114   Daniel, "Some Mortal Speculations," in *The Trail Home*, 199.

p. 114–15   Daniel, *Looking After: A Son's Memoir* (Washington, D.C.: Counterpoint Press, 1996), 251.

p. 115　　　Daniel, "A Word in Favor of Rootlessness,"
　　　　　　in *The Norton Book of Nature Writing,* 2nd ed.,
　　　　　　ed. Robert Finch and John Elder (New York:
　　　　　　W. W. Norton, 2002), 984–90.

p. 115–16　Daniel, *The Norton Book of Nature Writing,* 984.

p. 116　　　Daniel, *The Norton Book of Nature Writing,* 984.

p. 116　　　Daniel, *The Norton Book of Nature Writing,* 984.

p. 116–17　Daniel, *The Norton Book of Nature Writing,* 985.

p. 117　　　Daniel, *The Norton Book of Nature Writing,* 986.

p. 118　　　Daniel, *The Norton Book of Nature Writing,* 986.

p. 118　　　Daniel, *The Norton Book of Nature Writing,* 987.

p. 118　　　Daniel, *The Norton Book of Nature Writing,* 988.

p. 118　　　Daniel, *The Norton Book of Nature Writing,*
　　　　　　988–89.

p. 118–19　Daniel, *Oregon Rivers,* 159.

p. 119–20　Daniel, *Looking After,* 47.

p. 120　　　Daniel, *Looking After,* 43.

p. 121　　　Daniel, *Looking After,* 108.

p. 123　　　Daniel, preface to *The Sun Is Dancing Hot To-
　　　　　　night,* ed. John Daniel (limited edition student
　　　　　　chapbook, La Grande, Oreg., 1980).

p. 125　　　Daniel, preface to *Wild Song: Poems of the
　　　　　　Natural World,* ed. John Daniel (Athens: Uni-
　　　　　　versity of Georgia Press, 1998), xi.

p. 127　　　Daniel, untitled contribution to "Nature-
　　　　　　Writing Symposium," ed. John A. Murray,
　　　　　　Manoa (Fall 1992): 78.

p. 128   Daniel, *Oregon Rivers*, 159.

p. 129   Daniel, "Wallace Stegner, 1909–1993," in *The Trail Home*, 44.

p. 129   Scott H. Slovic and Terrell F. Dixon, eds., *Being in the World: An Environmental Reader for Writers* (New York: Macmillan, 1993), 84.

p. 130–31   Daniel, "Wallace Stegner's Hunger for Wholeness," in *Wallace Stegner and the Continental Vision: Essays on Literature, History, and Landscape,* ed. Curt Meine (Washington, D.C.: Island Press, 1997), 33.

p. 131   Stegner, *Wolf Willow: A History, a Story, and a Memory of the Last Plains Frontier* (New York: Viking, 1962), 3–4.

p. 132   Daniel, "The Unseen," in *All Things Touched by Wind* (Anchorage: Salmon Run Press, 1994), 45.

p. 134–35   Daniel, *Looking After,* 75–76.

SCOTT SLOVIC, founding president of the Association for the Study of Literature and Environment (ASLE), currently serves as editor of the journal *ISLE: Interdisciplinary Studies in Literature and Environment.* He is the author of *Seeking Awareness in American Nature Writing: Henry Thoreau, Annie Dillard, Edward Abbey, Wendell Berry, Barry Lopez* (University of Utah Press, 1992); his edited and coedited books include *Being in the World: An Environmental Reader for Writers* (Macmillan, 1993), *Reading the Earth: New Directions in the Study of Literature and the Environment* (University of Idaho Press, 1998), *Literature and the Environment: A Reader on Nature and Culture* (Addison Wesley Longman, 1999), and *Getting Over the Color Green: Contemporary Environmental Literature of the Southwest* (University of Arizona Press, 2001). He is currently professor of English at the University of Nevada, Reno, where he directed the Center for Environmental Arts and Humanities from 1995 to 2001.

MORE BOOKS ON THE WORLD AS HOME
FROM MILKWEED EDITIONS

To order books or for more information,
contact Milkweed at (800) 520-6455
or visit our website (www.worldashome.org).

The Credo *Series*

Brown Dog of the Yaak:
Essays on Art and Activism
Rick Bass

Writing the Sacred into the Real
Alison Hawthorne Deming

The Frog Run:
Words and Wildness in the Vermont Woods
John Elder

Taking Care:
Thoughts on Storytelling and Belief
William Kittredge

An American Child Supreme:
The Education of a Liberation Ecologist
John Nichols

Walking the High Ridge:
Life As Field Trip
Robert Michael Pyle

The Dream of the Marsh Wren:
Writing As Reciprocal Creation
Pattiann Rogers

The Country of Language
Scott Russell Sanders

Shaped by Wind and Water:
Reflections of a Naturalist
Ann Haymond Zwinger

Other World As Home Books

Wild Earth:
Wild Ideas for a World out of Balance
Edited by Tom Butler

The Book of the Everglades
Edited by Susan Cerulean

Swimming with Giants:
My Encounters with Whales, Dolphins, and Seals
Anne Collet

The Prairie in Her Eyes
Ann Daum

Boundary Waters:
The Grace of the Wild
Paul Gruchow

Grass Roots:
The Universe of Home
Paul Gruchow

The Necessity of Empty Places
Paul Gruchow

A Sense of the Morning:
Field Notes of a Born Observer
David Brendan Hopes

Arctic Refuge:
A Circle of Testimony
Compiled by Hank Lentfer and Carolyn Servid

This Incomparable Land:
A Guide to American Nature Writing
Thomas J. Lyon

A Wing in the Door:
Life with a Red-Tailed Hawk
Peri Phillips McQuay

The Barn at the End of the World:
The Apprenticeship of a Quaker, Buddhist Shepherd
Mary Rose O'Reilley

Ecology of a Cracker Childhood
Janisse Ray

Of Landscape and Longing:
Finding a Home at the Water's Edge
Carolyn Servid

The Book of the Tongass
Edited by Carolyn Servid and Donald Snow

Homestead
Annick Smith

Testimony:
Writers of the West Speak
On Behalf of Utah Wilderness
Compiled by Stephen Trimble and
Terry Tempest Williams

World As Home for Kids

Stories from Where We Live—The California Coast
Edited by Sara St. Antoine

Stories from Where We Live—
The Great North American Prairie
Edited by Sara St. Antoine

Stories from Where We Live—The North Atlantic Coast
Edited by Sara St. Antoine

THE WORLD AS HOME, the nonfiction publishing program of Milkweed Editions, is dedicated to exploring our relationship to the natural world. Not espousing any particular environmentalist or political agenda, these books are a forum for distinctive literary writing that not only alerts the reader to vital issues but offers personal testimonies to living harmoniously with other species in urban, rural, and wilderness communities.

MILKWEED EDITIONS publishes with the intention of making a humane impact on society, in the belief that literature is a transformative art uniquely able to convey the essential experiences of the human heart and spirit. To that end, Milkweed publishes distinctive voices of literary merit in handsomely designed, visually dynamic books, exploring the ethical, cultural, and esthetic issues that free societies need continually to address. Milkweed Editions is a not-for-profit press.

JOIN US

Since its genesis as *Milkweed Chronicle* in 1979, Milkweed has helped hundreds of emerging writers reach their readers. Thanks to the generosity of foundations and individuals like you, Milkweed Editions is able to continue its nonprofit mission of publishing books chosen on the basis of literary merit—of how they impact the human heart and spirit—rather than on how they impact the bottom line. That's a miracle that our readers have made possible.

In addition to purchasing Milkweed books, you can join the growing community of Milkweed supporters. Individual contributions of any amount are both meaningful and welcome. Contact us for a Milkweed catalog or log on to www.milkweed.org and click on "About Milkweed," then "Why Join Milkweed," to find out about our donor program, or simply call 800-520-6455 and ask about becoming one of Milkweed's contributors. As a nonprofit press, Milkweed belongs to you, the community. Milkweed's board, its staff, and especially the authors whose careers you help launch thank you for reading our books and supporting our mission in any way you can.

Typeset in Stone Serif
by Stanton Publication Services, Inc.
Printed on acid-free, recycled
55# Frasier Miami Book Natural paper
by Friesen Corporation.